Nick Moseley

Nick Moseley was born in Trinidad in 1962, the son of a clergyman, and educated at Bristol Grammar School and Royal Holloway, University of London. He worked as an actor in the 1980s before entering the teaching profession in 1990. In 1997 he became Course Director of the BA (Hons) Acting programme at Italia Conti, where he began to develop his theories and training methodologies. Nick began teaching Meisner Technique in 2000. In 2006 he became a Senior Lecturer in Acting at Central School of Speech and Drama, where he has continued his Meisner teaching and research. His first book, *Acting and Reacting: Tools for the Modern Actor*, is also published by Nick Hern Books. He has three children and lives with his partner and family in Buckinghamshire.

Also by Nick Moseley

ACTING AND REACTING:
TOOLS FOR THE MODERN ACTOR

Nick Moseley

MEISNER
in Practice

A Guide for Actors, Directors and Teachers

NICK HERN BOOKS
London
www.nickhernbooks.co.uk

A Nick Hern Book

Meisner in Practice
first published in Great Britain in 2012
by Nick Hern Books Limited,
The Glasshouse, 49a Goldhawk Road, London W12 8QP

Reprinted 2014

Cover designed by Nick Hern Books
Cover image © robodread,
used under licence from Shutterstock.com

Typeset by Nick Hern Books
Printed and bound in Great Britain by
T.J. International, Padstow, Cornwall

A CIP catalogue record for this book is available
from the British Library

ISBN 978 1 84842 087 8

Contents

Foreword

Sanford Meisner, actor and actor trainer, was born in Brooklyn in 1905, and from the early 1930s until the 1990s taught acting in New York, first at the Group Theatre alongside Lee Strasberg and Stella Adler, and later at the Actors Studio and the Neighbourhood Playhouse. He continued teaching at the Playhouse until a few years before his death in 1997.

Meisner's work, like Strasberg's, derives from the theory and practice of Konstantin Stanislavsky, but unlike Strasberg, Meisner places emphasis on truthful interaction between actors in imaginary circumstances rather than on searching one's own past for emotions or sensations in order to find a connection with the character.

Over the years, Meisner Technique evolved into a detailed training process which has been documented by former colleagues and students, and which is still practised worldwide by a variety of practitioners, many of whom studied with Meisner himself.

The purpose of this book is to offer students and practitioners a detailed theoretical and practical account of the most useful aspects of Meisner Technique, based both on reports of Meisner's own practice and on my own reflections and observations while teaching this technique over a period of more than ten years.

While being an enthusiastic proponent of many aspects of this technique, I do not see it as a complete actor-training process in itself, but as an essential part of more comprehensive training programmes – and as a useful complement to Stanislavsky-based training elements.

Through description, analysis and practical example, I will attempt to take the reader through various stages of Meisner training, including the pitfalls and problems that I have encountered in my own teaching of the technique. At points I will also explain how I have adapted some of the exercises to make them work better, or faster.

My hope is that in the fullness of time, Meisner Technique will cease to be seen as something separate, alternative or self-contained, and will become more integrated into the broader canon of actor-training processes, where I believe it will be of immense value.

Nick Moseley

1

The Need for Meisner

'The foundation of acting is the reality of doing'

The Need for Meisner

During the latter part of the twentieth century, as film and television have gradually taken over from live theatre as the most popular form of drama, there has been an ever-increasing demand within the English-speaking world for actors to be more 'real'. With the camera able to capture every gesture, reaction and thought in high definition, the heightened and rather gestural acting style of the early-twentieth-century theatre now appears laughably stilted and out of date, despite its claim to be 'naturalistic'.

The term 'real', when we apply it to acting today, now implies a deeper and fuller immersion of the actor, both in the role and in the world of the play. It also implies – just as significantly – a more organic and immediate connection to the other actors, so that what the audience sees and hears is not just a theatrical retelling of a dialogue, but an actual and present event in which the real and involuntary physical and vocal reactions of the actors to one another seduce (rather than cajole) the audience into suspending their disbelief.

There is actually no such thing as realism in drama, if by realism we mean something that accurately reproduces real life.

Real life is chaotic, confused and unbounded, while actors naturally seek to give their work clarity, meaning and form. What passes for realism in any era depends on the taste and sensibility of the audiences. In each era we have a slightly different understanding of what we mean by realistic acting, in the sense that we may find some acting convincing, gripping and moving, and other acting (which might possibly have impressed our ancestors) contrived, stilted and inorganic. Today's actors are therefore required to do whatever it takes to make the audience *feel* they are experiencing something real.

In this age of the camera, and indeed of the small, intimate auditorium, everything has tended towards a more detailed and believable (if not actually more accurate) representation of life in all its disorder and mess. Writers of gritty modern realism often try to recreate the disjointed, repetitious, overlapping dialogue of real life. Actors no longer get to finish their characters' sentences or complete their thoughts. In modern-day realism, the rhythm of the text depends not on whichever actor happens to be speaking, but on the way two or more actors get into rhythm with one another.

If actors are to do this, they have to give up some measure of control. They still can, and must, work very hard on preparing a role, yet both in rehearsal and performance they need to find a connection with their scene partners so that, moment to moment, it is not just the choices made in rehearsal, but the real-life reactions of one human being to another, which dictate how the actor speaks, thinks and moves.

To train an actor to do this might seem remarkably simple. After all, we talk easily and naturally to one another all the time in real life, and we effortlessly allow ourselves to respond organically to the ebb and flow of the conversation. To do this as actors, however, is much harder. In a drama we are usually working not with our own words, but with a text written by someone else. We find it hard to accept the idea that someone else's text can possibly emerge spontaneously from our mouths in response to a real moment that we have experienced. As the text is contrived by a writer, we reason, so must the motivation for speaking it be contrived by the director and actors in rehearsal. So we don't engage with the other actor as we would in real life, because we assume that we already have everything we need to deliver what is required of us. We do, of course, require the physical presence of the other actor so that our lines can be spoken to someone, and so that our cues can be received in the right order, but nothing is actually being negotiated – it has all been agreed beforehand!

Ten years ago I was struggling with this problem within my own acting classes. We were using tried-and-tested Stanislavskian techniques based on the Method of Physical Action. Our actors were building their inner life, and they understood the landscape of the play and their own scenes. Yet it seemed that whatever method we used and however well the actors were prepared, some key element was lacking in the end product. There was something false, contrived, about the dialogues, even when they made perfect sense, as if the actors were musicians playing well, but just ever so slightly out of time with each other. It was hard to define – it just felt wrong. In other words, we didn't quite believe that the conversation was happening in front of us. It was more like a re-enactment of a conversation that had happened at another time, in another place, which was being replayed to us to give us a broad idea of what the conversation was and how it looked and sounded.

Of course, we knew what the problem was. Everyone has the ability to have 'real' conversations which are truly in the 'here and now', but when we do this in our own lives, we have no text and we (usually) have a personal reason for being in the conversation. What we say in each moment, and how we say it, cannot be decided other than through our understanding of the moment and our reading of the other person. If the other person is talkative, we may be searching for a moment to get a word in edgeways; if they are monosyllabic, we may be trying to stimulate them to a more enlivened response. We don't know what they are going to say, or how they will say it, and we are responsive to the smallest changes in them that tell us how they are hearing us.

The actor who has learned his lines and worked on his character, however, is in a very different place. He knows that whatever he may observe and understand in the moment of performance, the words he and his scene partners speak will still be the words of the play, and the outcome of the scene will not change. This means that the motivation to listen to his fellow actor and genuinely respond – cognitively and physically – to what he observes, is much weaker than his motivation to 'act well', which in this case probably means to speak clearly and perform the lines and moves with accuracy and conviction.

Ironically, of course, by not responding to the other actor in a natural, unforced way, the actor unwittingly *stops* himself from acting well. His work may be crisp, well-formed, clear in motivation and meaning, he may make use of an impressive vocal and physical range, and he may even be emotionally available – but somehow we won't quite believe him.

In my attempts to train my actors to respond to each other on this level, I have always reminded them that no matter how much is fixed within a production, there is always space for the actor's creativity, by which I mean the creative, impulsive response of the actor to his fellow actor. Even if the play has been blocked down to the last move and gesture, there should be variations in the way the actor experiences each performance, however minute and apparently imperceptible.

Many actors seem to forget this. They assume that their job is to inhabit what has been set, rather than to use what has been set as a basis from which they can focus on the relationship with the other actor. Moreover, even if they do realise the value of that moment-to-moment connection, many find it very hard to achieve it. This is because, although they have trained their bodies and voices to be clear, uncluttered and heightened performative signifiers, in so doing they have lost the ability to remain open and flexible, and to be continually and unconsciously adjusting to their surroundings.

There are two reasons for this. The first is that, in real life, this process of continual adjustment can manifest itself as fidgeting, shifting – physical and vocal 'ers' and 'ums' – which can have the effect of dispersing energy and cluttering the audience's experience with excess information. This is exactly what the training has taught the actor not to do. The second reason is that when the trained body, with its open breath and released musculature, starts to become responsive to other similarly trained bodies, there can be startling emotional responses, which the actor may find quite uncomfortable, and therefore seek to avoid.

The blocks thereby created are hard to remove: just *wanting* to remove them is not enough. Acting teachers and directors use many techniques to get actors to respond more organically to one another, including different forms of physical improvisation. For example, if two actors are working on a scene which involves them in a verbal or intellectual conflict, they can start a rehearsal exploring the physical/visceral side of the conflict by pitting their physical strength against each other, and then play the scene with the physical memory of that conflict still present in the body. These exercises can work very well – they get the breath deeper into the body and allow the actor to feel a new intensity and a heightened connection to other actors. Unfortunately, the effects tend to be short-lived, because the moment the physical memory fades, so, usually, does this feeling.

The Meisner Technique, provided it is pursued relentlessly over an extended period of time, can offer a solution. Within

7

clear structures and safe exercises, it slowly and methodically reconditions the habits of the actor, bridging the gap between real life and the acting space, and slowly but surely shifting the 'default' setting of the actor from 'closed' to 'open'. Little by little it removes the fear of the moment, so that the actor learns to make his trained body open and responsive, despite the emotional risk.

The beauty of the technique lies in its simplicity and its insistence on genuine, truthful responses. If well-taught, it can permanently affect the way an actor works in the space, often without the actor really being conscious of the changes taking place.

However, like most actor-training techniques, it cannot be applied indiscriminately or simply delivered as a package. As Meisner himself was aware, the process is endlessly diagnostic, and each actor engaging in it has to be side-coached and nurtured through each stage, otherwise the work can result in little more than confusion and frustration.

This book is therefore devoted to an exploration of what the techniques are, how the exercises work practically, and how the acting teacher guides his students through the process and ensures that effective learning takes place.

2 The First Exercise

'What you do doesn't depend on you – it depends on the other fellow'

The First Exercise

Repetition exercises are probably the most memorable and unique aspects of Meisner Technique. I do not think they have any equivalent within the whole canon of actor-training exercises. They are designed to strip away the artificiality of the theatre and return you to one of your most basic human abilities – to receive and respond to messages from others, and to allow the actions of others to be the principal determinant of how you yourselves act.

Most of the repetition exercises described in the first half of this book would have belonged in the first year of an original Meisner training programme. Meisner classes build and develop from simple exercises to much more complex ones, the idea being that the habits ingrained at the start of the training are carried forward into scene work and performance. While I would seek to maintain this trajectory within a Meisner programme, I would also make one proviso. I do not believe that an actor can get the best out of even the simplest of these exercises without at least a year of prior training, in voice, movement, concentration, stamina and articulation, amongst other skills.

For this reason I have never attempted to introduce Meisner into the curriculum before the second year of a three-year programme. Actors need some basic skills and habits in place before they start this work, otherwise it can become head-based, emotionally disconnected and lacking in energy.

Early repetition exercises often take place on chairs, with two actors sitting facing each other and remaining seated throughout the whole exercise. There are no characters, no story, no script, no props other than the clothes the actors are wearing. There is nothing to hide behind – no masks, no assumed gestures, no beautiful language, no stylistic quality. There is nothing except the actors themselves.

This may sound very exposing, and on one level it is, but you shouldn't make the mistake of assuming that just because the trappings of the theatre are absent, this is therefore any more real, as a situation, than a scene from a play. A repetition exercise is as fictional as any other encounter that takes place within the theatrical space, and therefore should operate with the same boundaries and the same level of personal 'safety'. The fiction lies not in imaginary worlds and stories, but in the fact that the relationship set up with the other actor, and everything that takes place within it, belongs to the exercise and not to the real world. If you can trust in this, you will be free – if you doubt it, then fear will hold you back.

(In all the examples in Chapters 2–6, the participating actors appear to be male, but this is for convenience only, and in each example, one or both of the actors could just as easily be female.)

Before starting the first Meisner exercise, I normally ask all the actors in the room to pair off and practise sitting opposite one another and just looking, without words, for several minutes at a time. In each pair, I ask them to number themselves as Actor 1 and Actor 2. For a few minutes, both actors in each pair have the task of just looking at the other. The results are usually predictable and fairly consistent. Among other things, I observe:

- Laughter, mainly through shared embarrassment, but sometimes where one actor makes silly faces to entertain the other, or both set up a kind of amused complicity.

- Status levels, where one actor becomes the observer and the other the observed.

- Boredom, where the actors switch off from one another, or let their attention wander to other pairs.

- Staring games, where one or both actors try to intimidate the other.

- Trances, where one or both actors get locked into a kind of hypnotic eye contact.

When I ask actors to talk about their experiences, it often emerges that they feel very uncomfortable being observed, and employ one or more of the above tactics to try to avoid the feeling of exposure. This is perfectly understandable, and I tell them so. Even trainee actors, about to embark on a career that is all about being looked at, rarely feel comfortable being observed in this way – out of role, devoid of activity or words.

In the next stage of the exercise, I tell each pair that Actor 1 is the observer, Actor 2 the observed. This time the Actor 1s are completely different. Although some still laugh at times, most of them are now attentive, relaxed and purposeful. The Actor 2s, by contrast, are self-conscious, embarrassed and giggly. They close their body language, shift uncomfortably and fidget. One very high-status Actor 2 refuses to accept the role of the observed, and tries to intimidate his partner.

After a while I switch round, allowing Actor 2 to be the observer, and the same thing happens in reverse. Finally, I tell them that they are both in role as observers, and interestingly, although a certain amount of self-consciousness creeps back in at times, most actors manage to keep the focus off themselves and on their partner, at least for a while. After a few minutes, however, there is simply not enough to occupy the actors' attention, and it begins to wander.

The point of all this, as most actors agree, is that it doesn't matter who is watching you, provided you are not watching yourself, or even watching someone watching you. In other words, if you can train yourself to keep the focus elsewhere, and stay relaxed, you can avoid the tension which so often creeps into your body and stops you being responsive, released and real.

Meisner exercises offer both a reason for keeping that focus away from yourself, and a simple ongoing task that keeps the relationship alive, dynamic and changing, so that you don't ever have to get bored or lose focus.

Mechanical Repetition

In the first exercise, you and another actor sit on chairs facing each other, at a distance from one another that allows you to see not just the face of your partner, but their whole body. After a while, one of you makes a simple statement about something you notice about the other actor. This will be a physical, irrefutable fact, such as 'red socks'. The other actor repeats the phrase back to you exactly as you have said it, copying your intonation, volume and pronunciation exactly. You then do the same, repeating not what you think you said the first time, but what you *hear from the other actor*, and so it goes on until the teacher stops the exercise.

With this understanding, you can embark on the first and simplest of the Meisner repetition exercises.

The purpose of this exercise is to create a situation in which your only guiding principle in moving the encounter forward is the instruction to reproduce what you hear as exactly as possible. This forces you to listen and to process, so that what emerges is directly influenced by the stimulus the other actor has given you. This is the first step in allowing the other actor, rather than yourself, to determine your actions.

The beauty of the first exercise lies in its simplicity. It is a task that is well within your scope and yet requires enough of your attention to keep you interested and engaged. Each moment is different from the last, and each moment influences the next moment.

Example 1

The first time we do the exercise, it starts well, but after a while I stop it and ask the group why I have stopped. One or two of the sharper ones have spotted the problem. The phrase Actor 1 started with was 'green shirt', and the intonation we heard was quite chirpy and enthusiastic, a quality Actor 2 heard and tried to reproduce. As a group, however, we were able to hear the differences between the way Actor 1 spoke the phrase and how Actor 2 repeated it. That in itself was not a problem, because Actor 2 was genuinely trying to repeat what he heard.

What Actor 1 then did was to repeat, not Actor 2's intonation, but his own initial offer. This happened several times, and we were left with the impression of a teacher trying to correct a not very able pupil.

Actor 1 is surprised to have this pointed out, and (because some people within the group seem very pleased with themselves for spotting the error) a little put out and defensive. I remind the group that everyone will be doing the exercise at some point, and that their observations need to be supportive. What this has shown us is that within the acting space we like to find ways of maintaining status and control, probably in order to counter our fear and sense of exposure. We do this unconsciously, as a habit, which means that we must consciously seek to undo it.

We start again, this time with a comment from Actor 2 – 'brown eyes'. After about eight or nine exchanges I stop it again, and most of the group can see the problem. Actor 1 has been trying to reproduce what he hears, but because there are people watching he has tended to over-articulate, to demonstrate his reproduction rather than simply doing it. It is almost as if he wants to show the group how good he is at picking up the nuances of what he hears, but the result is actually inaccurate because it is heightened and exaggerated. By performing his ability to do the task he is not actually doing it – rather he is commenting on it. I ask both actors to take the performance out of the work and just carry out the task. We start again with 'wavy hair'.

This time, each tries hard to reproduce what he hears rather than pushing his own version or commenting. We do get some genuine responses, but after only a few exchanges the phrase becomes quieter and more mumbled, until it is virtually inaudible. Once again we stop. Once again I consult the group to find out what went wrong.

The answer comes back that neither actor seemed particularly bothered. It is certainly true that each time they repeated it, the phrase lost a little more of its initial energy, but I suspect there has been no conscious desire to undermine or disrespect the exercise. It is just that the task seems so small, so lacking in drama, that they have unconsciously made the choice to work with low energy. In particular, they are not breathing as actors, which means that the voices lack resonance and power, and the bodies are not engaged. The exercise has become 'head-bound' and consequently the actors, and we, have lost interest.

I now ask the group why they think that the forward energy, commitment and emotional engagement of the actors is so lacking in this moment. The answer comes back loud and clear. They are unable to commit because they have no emotional investment. Stripped of the slightly competitive approach they took the first time round, they have become demotivated, bored and disconnected. In other words, despite having a simple task to perform, neither actually wants anything from the other actor.

For me this is a first principle of all repetition exercises – there must be a level of engagement with the other actor, or the exercises quickly become meaningless. If you are told to improvise a scene in character, the story usually provides you with an objective that is strong enough to lift your energy, support your voice and engage your body in what you are doing. The problem with the simpler repetition exercises is that you have no story, no objective, not even a character to give you those permissions. On one level you are too bored to engage because you can't see what's in it for you; on another level you are too scared to engage because you would be engaging as yourself.

Your Stanislavskian training has taught you that the objective is the primary motivator of the actor. It clarifies and lends meaning to every word spoken, every event experienced. It energises you, heightens your perceptions, and creates a connection to the other actor. Without it you are stripped firstly of desire and secondly of permission. To engage with someone from whom you want nothing feels false – at best a social game, at worst a social gaffe.

But what if I say to you that despite its lack of fictional circumstances, characters and situations, the acting space in which you do the repetition exercises is still a fictional space? What is more, because it is so, you can find within it a fictional objective which requires neither character nor backstory, and which will confer upon the actors the permissions of the fictional world.

The fiction you employ here is simple, easy to believe in, and consistent with the actor's exploratory persona. It is this: in this world, which consists of two chairs in a space, the other actor is *the most important person in your life*, partly because there is no one else, and partly because within the nature of the task, he or she is the sole determinant of your next act – the repetition of the chosen phrase – and the sole recipient of that act. Everything you do is because of, and for, the other actor.

Your objective is therefore 'I want to know this person better.' The reason you have this objective is because the other actor is not only the only person other than yourself in this world, but is to a large extent an unknown and unpredictable quantity.

The given circumstances are that you are sitting facing each other on two chairs on which you have to stay seated, and that you can only converse by reproducing in every detail exactly what the other person says.

That's all very well, you may say, but exactly how can I pursue my objective when I am thus restricted? Many of the strategies you might have used to further a relationship – including language, physical contact and specific gestures – are closed to you. My response to you is that *all* encounters between two human beings are played out within specific and often restrictive circumstances. Two people trying to speak over loud music, or while travelling on a crowded bus, or while dancing a waltz, might experience equivalent problems. There are many situations in which you might feel frustration at these restrictions, where your objective cries out for more scope and freedom, yet very often it is the acceptance of those circumstances that allows you to make the most of what you have. You cannot always be 'pushing' towards your objective in the most direct and obvious way – sometimes you simply have to follow the steps and trust.

Mechanical Repetition forces you to think about the objective not in terms of yourself but in terms of the other actor. Your objective, if you can call it that, is to reproduce exactly what your partner says, and if you follow that instruction to the letter, you will discover that the only way you can fulfil the task is by listening with your body, bypassing the judgemental, analytical part of your brain (which only gets in the way) and allowing the body to mirror your partner's, so it is not just the sound but their whole presence to which you are responding.

Reproducing within a less tense and yet more intense environment, you start to 'breathe in' the other actor and accept his or her presence on a deeper level. We the audience can hear that, beneath the simplicity of the words 'red socks' or 'brown hair', there is subtext and an unspoken need for connection, which manifests itself in the desire to reproduce what you hear. You have begun to understand Meisner.

3

Simple Repetition

'You've got control over what you're saying and I say *he* has to have control'

Simple Repetition

The move from Mechanical to Simple Repetition is a slight one in terms of the rules and circumstances, but it is a massive leap for the actor. In this 'simple' version of the exercise, the actor has to give up even more conscious control and allow the other actor to dictate his responses. In the process, most actors come up against their own barriers and defence mechanisms, sometimes for the first time.

Simple Repetition

The basic set-up is the same as before – you and your partner sit on two chairs facing each other. Once again you look at each other from head to toe. Once again a comment emerges from one of you, but this time it is personalised: '*You have* red socks,' or '*You've got a* black jumper.' This time, the second actor repeats the phrase back in a reversed form. '*I have* red socks,' or '*I've got a* black jumper,' so that the comment continues to be about the same thing and, as importantly, continues to be true.

In this exercise, however, you should make no attempt to reproduce the intonation of what you hear. You repeat the words, and you try to do so in a way which is open, responsive and organic to the situation. In other words, you do not impose anything on your response, but you allow the other person to affect the way in which your response comes out.

It should also be emphasised here that, whatever phrase is chosen, the actors should not attach too much literal significance to the socks, the jumper, or whatever. The significance must therefore lie in the *subtext*, which is often not about the black jumper itself but about the actual interaction taking place, whatever that may be.

The comments should also avoid any 'in-jokes' or concealed meanings within the chosen comment, which lie outside of the space, because they rely on the two actors' own knowledge of one another; otherwise the exercise becomes about the real lives of the participants, which is not the object.

By the time you start Simple Repetition you will have become quite adept at observing and analysing the work of other actors. This is important, because in Meisner work you will learn a great deal from observing others. It is often difficult to spot your problems while you are actually doing the exercises, but if you watch others intently and find ways of describing what you see, this will help you understand and accept what others say about you.

Example 1

The first pair starts the exercise with a simple factual comment, yet they fall almost immediately into one of the more common errors. I stop them, look expectantly over at the group, and am immediately told what the problem is. The two actors have sat down, looked at one another and, in a tacit yet entirely complicit way, agreed on their respective roles before even a word is spoken. Here we have the stern schoolteacher and the meek pupil. The schoolteacher chooses the line 'Your ears are pierced,' the pupil responds accordingly with 'My ears are pierced,' and already the roles and the story are fixed. Both actors seem comfortable with these roles and the whole thing quickly gets stuck in that transaction.

A1   (*Firm and authoritative.*) Your ears are pierced.

A2   (*Surprised, unaware it was a problem.*) My ears are pierced.

A1   (*Spelling it out.*) Your ears are pierced.

A2   (*Embarrassed.*) My ears are pierced.

A1   (*Accusing.*) Your ears are pierced.

A2   (*Apologising.*) My ears are pierced.

A1   (*Scolding.*) Your ears are pierced.

A2   (*Repentant.*) My ears are pierced.

A1   (*Furious.*) Your ears are pierced!

A2   (*Grovelling.*) My ears are pierced.

A1   (*Dismissive.*) Your ears are pierced.

A2   (*Seeking forgiveness.*) My ears are pierced.

A1   (*Making the best of a bad situation.*) Your ears are pierced.

The story thus played out is comprehensible and entertaining, but it is not real. It is a safe little improvised playlet, whose parameters are clear and immovable from the start. By assuming these status roles, both actors have ensured that they will not have to operate outside of the preordained transaction. It might of course have been possible for Actor 2 to challenge the authority of Actor 1, but such a move lies beyond her personal permissions, and she shies away from it.

The group is, of course, already familiar with that particular kind of role-play from both partners. Actor 1 is a leading force within the group, a motivator and disciplinarian. Actor 2 is playing out a meeker and more submissive role, which the group has seen many times before in different contexts. What this has highlighted, as I point out to the group, is the extent to which trainee actors' fixed status roles within the group, whether in a three-year conservatoire programme or a six-week evening class, can seep into the work and determine their responses to one another in a way that predetermines and ultimately restricts the exercises. 'But I'm naturally submissive,' protests one. 'I can be bold when I'm playing a character but this is just me.'

This raises significant questions about the nature of character within drama. If you, the actor, have no permissions beyond those conferred upon you by the playwright and the director, then must it not be that the character will always sit outside you? The wonderful thing about the acting space is surely that, within it, there are many permissions offered to each and every actor, which allow you to explore outside of your 'comfort zone'. Thus the submissive actor becomes dominant, the dominant becomes vulnerable, not because the stage direction says '*She shouts*' or '*He is close to tears*', but because to do so is exciting and liberating. If you can remind yourselves that the Meisner space is still fictional, still an actor's space, you can start to allow the same permissions to operate here.

However, within this exercise you are not trying specifically to explore the flip sides of your everyday persona. You are merely trying to be open to whatever possibility arises within a context that asks you to make choices as easily and organically as you breathe. At first it may be hard to distinguish between a choice that is defined by habit and conditioning, and one that is a simpler – more spontaneous – response to what you see and hear in the other actor. It is something that is easier to spot from outside than to feel in yourself, as actors frequently comment. But the more you do the exercise, the better you understand.

Example 1 continued

Actor 2 opens with 'You've got black hair.' This time, in an effort not to impose a status relationship from outside, Actor 1 becomes expressionless and wooden. He repeats in a muttered monotone, keeping the body still, and 'downward inflecting' each repetition so that it implies a wish to close down and terminate the encounter rather than continue and develop the relationship.

Quickly, rather than embark upon another lengthy discussion, I remind him of the objective from the last exercise and ask him to work with it in this exercise. Clearly, if you want to gain a knowledge of someone else that goes deeper than their public persona, you need to offer something different from your own public persona. This is true of most relationships – change can only occur if both parties are prepared to step away from the safety of their accepted roles. How that 'stepping away' takes place, however, cannot be planned, but is dependent on the moment-to-moment nature of the exchange.

This time, Actor 1 starts to work in a more open, vulnerable way, softening his tone in a way that is genuinely open to his partner rather than manipulative. Unfortunately, his partner slips immediately into another role, this time that of client in a counselling session, which forces Actor 1 into the high-status counsellor role. His tone continues to be gentle and reassuring, but it is no longer vulnerable. Once again we are stuck. This time, I remind Actor 2 that the objective is two-way, and that he too needs to be active within the exercise.

After several false starts, both actors start to work more flexibly with one another, as though they are both striving to keep the 'ball' of their relationship constantly in the air and constantly changing. Because Actor 2 is no longer submissive and vulnerable by default, he ceases to be the 'subject' of the conversation, and he turns the focus onto Actor 1 rather than himself.

What happens then surprises the group. All of a sudden, within the repeated exchanges, Actor 1 starts to become emotional. I murmur 'keep going' to ensure that this doesn't make him step out of the relationship, and the repetition continues. The moment of crisis passes, but Actor 2 is deeply affected. He starts to treat Actor 1 with 'kid gloves', clearly worried in case he triggers another such reaction. Actor 1 notices this, and his tone communicates to Actor 2 that it's all right, he feels okay now. And all on the phrase 'You have a black T-shirt...' 'I have a black T-shirt.'

I allow all of this because it is not imposed – it arises naturally from the relationship within this space at this time and absorbs one hundred per cent of the actors' attention. The group no longer exists. It is only when the relationship starts to 'plateau' and the actors' attention to wander slightly, that I stop them, but they have done well.

Example 2

The next couple have a slightly different problem, one that is perhaps more deeply ingrained and harder to deal with. Here the issue is not so much the respective status roles of the two actors within the group, as the actors' long-standing habits and defence mechanisms, which operate regardless of who the other actor is. Actor 3 is habitually reserved, watchful, as if continually expecting to be attacked. Actor 4 by contrast operates with blank neutrality, appearing relaxed and unbothered, yet never registering on the outside any of the reactions we suspect are taking place within.

The result is a lifeless stalemate, which quickly grinds to a halt. Having heard the group's analysis of what they have seen, which largely accords with my own observations, I remind both actors once again of the agreed objective, and suggest to them that their respective versions of the 'closed', default position may be working against their stated intention: 'I want to gain a deeper knowledge of this person.'

In the discussion that follows, it emerges that both actors have difficulty, even in scripted work, with being 'on the front foot', in the sense of committing to an intention and allowing themselves to be responsive and vulnerable in the pursuit of something. Neither actor lacks intelligence or the ability to understand the demands of a text, but ingrained within both is a physical and psychological reluctance to yield control within the acting space to any other actor. It is not even a conscious decision, but a habit possibly dating back many years and relating to real-life spaces which were indeed unsafe.

I reiterate to these actors that the purpose of these exercises, amongst other things, is to highlight such habits and ultimately to help shift them. I add that the rules and given circumstances we apply are not supposed to be threatening or scary, but are simple steps which actors can use to help them make new and different choices. Within the discussion we arrive at a place where both actors understand this and are determined to make changes.

We start again, on the phrase 'You've got small hands.' This time the group is watching intently, clocking every reaction, every pause, every stifling of the breath; noting any fidgeting, shifting, avoidance. I allow the group to stop the exercise if they see persistent evasions or defensive tactics. After a few stops the actors begin to work in a way that is less closed, more responsive and with a greater sense of investment in each other.

Actor 3 gets there more quickly. It appears that with a slight shift in energy and a certain releasing of muscular and facial tension he can very quickly move to a much more vulnerable place. He becomes very open, enlivened and interested in his partner.

Actor 4 takes longer. With him it is less a matter of releasing tension than of allowing his body and voice to register, however slightly, his inner life. This is hard for him – it is almost as if the wiring for this process simply isn't there. His voice is resonant yet monotone, his body released yet completely motionless.

In one of our pauses I remind him of one of Meisner's fundamental principles regarding text, which is that the text, whether scripted or improvised, should be like 'a canoe floating on the river of the action'. In other words, it is the series of moments within the relationship that are important, not the words themselves. You know already that the words of this particular text are not in themselves of great significance, but provided that the actors are responsive to one another, constantly open to being affected by the other's voice and physical presence, then the spoken text can become an outward sign of the inner journey, not through the words, which are unchanging, but through the minute variations in pitch, tone, volume and stress.

Actor 4 understands perfectly, but says he simply cannot imagine how to make his body and voice responsive to his inner experience without contriving and faking. I advise him to take the focus off himself and place it firmly back onto Actor 3. I also remind him about the objective.

ME   So, are you achieving your objective?

A4   Yes, I think I am.

ME   Tell me what you mean by that.

A4   Well, he's getting more open – less defensive.

ME   Is that enough for you?

A4   (*After a moment's thought.*) No... no, it isn't.

At this point they resume the exercise. I could have pushed the questions further, but I feel that Actor 4 has already understood that, without commitment and openness from him, Actor 3 will eventually back off and shut down.

The change we see is slight but significant. Actor 4 is naturally truthful and does not try to fool us. It is not possible for him to make his body expressive and responsive overnight, after years of practising the opposite. However, he is now committing to the objective and directing his focus and concentration towards Actor 3. We begin to hear changes in his voice, and at the same time we start to see impulses in the body, not followed through, but in stark contrast to the blank canvas we were previously looking at. Actor 3 picks up on these changes, and finally they achieve a genuine interaction. It doesn't go as far as it could, but for these two actors it's a start.

By this time, everyone in the group has understood, some for the first time, what we are trying to achieve. It is hard to *quantify* the difference between the experience of watching two actors performing for an audience and the experience of watching two people genuinely engaged with one another, yet it is very easy to *know* the difference as an observer. Little by little, the group is inspired to engage with the exercise and explore its possibilities.

It may take several sessions, but if you keep on doing Simple Repetition you will almost certainly manage, after a few stops and starts, to relinquish control sufficiently to let a much more spontaneous reactivity happen than you were prepared to allow at the start. For the most part, these changes are achieved through the following simple psycho-physical choices:

- Breathing into a released torso.
- Maintaining a sense of connection and shared energy with the other actor.
- Resisting the temptation to control and manipulate.
- Focusing on and being interested in the other actor.

The purpose of Simple Repetition is to take you back to the most basic kind of verbal and visual interplay, so that you can experience what it means to observe and respond without the fictional characters, dramatic stories or intense dialogue which you have come to expect and which can so easily become substitutes for genuine interaction.

Some of you may find it more difficult than others to let go of habits and fixed role-play, even when you have arrived – through many hours of observation – at a very full understanding of the difference between organic interaction and contrived theatricality. There is a simple preparatory exercise that you can use to achieve a more open body and released breath, which takes persistence and patience, but which can help actors 'crack' Simple Repetition.

Stage One

You stand facing your partner (without the group watching) and each of you starts to breathe with a slow regular rhythm, taking the breath in through the nose and out through the mouth.

You now start to 'gesture' the breath. On the out-breath, your hands and arms gesture towards your partner as if conducting the breath towards them. On the in-breath, the hands 'gather' the breath back into your body.

Gradually, the two of you find a rhythm with one another so that while one is breathing out the other breathes in. The effect is that you are 'breathing in' your partner and they are 'breathing in' you. On a literal level, you are breathing their air; on a metaphorical level it is as though you are breathing a kind of 'essence' of them.

Once the rhythm has become established, and you have both adapted yourselves to it, taking in just enough air to sustain the rhythm, you can start to add a sound – usually at this stage a continuous, sung 'ma-a-a-a' sound which accords with the open mouth. As you breathe in, you allow your body to inhale the sound made by your partner, so that you are hearing it not just with your ears but with your whole body.

Having relaxed into this new exchange, you and your partner can start to alter the sound, keeping it as a continuous, sung sound but altering the pitch, volume and vowel sound and throwing in further consonants, the effect being a little like an Islamic call to prayer.

Both you and your partner now start to allow your choices on the sound to be affected and shaped both by what you hear and by what you see, so that the stimulus for changes comes only from the relationship and not from personal inventiveness. You can also allow your gestures on both the out-breath and the in-breath to be affected and shaped by the sounds, although the gestures retain their essential qualities of 'offering' and 'receiving'.

Once you have reached this level of interaction, it is possible to continue the exercise almost indefinitely. It is essential that the sounds remain part of a dialogue and do not become a duet, although it is likely that within the dialogue there will be a certain overlapping as one sound comes in over the end of another.

Having taught the body to be open to abstract sounds, you may now be able to 'transfer' the feeling of physical responsiveness to a Simple Repetition exercise. In the end, success in Simple Repetition is just a small but significant act of relinquishing control.

It is only when you have learned to maintain focus on the other actor, to keep relaxed and to keep breathing no matter what happens, that you will be ready to move on.

4

Standard Repetition

'Don't do anything unless something happens to make you do it'

Standard Repetition

Standard Repetition is much more daunting than Simple Repetition because in this form of the exercise you are confronted not merely with the need for an open, unforced response to your partner, but with the inescapable fact that someone is not only looking intently at you, but also noticing and commenting on much of what you do.

Standard Repetition
Working in pairs, sitting on the chairs exactly as before, you comment on your partner exactly as in Simple Repetition. The difference, in this version, is that each of you is now free to *change* the comment if and when you see your partner doing something significant. For example:

A1	You have dark hair.
A2	I have dark hair.
A1	You have dark hair.

A2	I have dark hair.
A1	You touched your hair.
A2	I touched my hair.
A1	You touched your hair.
A2	You sat forward.
A1	I sat forward.

Each comment is repeated continuously, as in Simple Repetition, until something happens to change it. You will also notice that all comments relating to physical actions are made in the past tense, so that they never stop being true. At this stage, the comments all have to be physical, factual and irrefutable.

You must repeat every comment made about you at least once and preferably more than once. You should not look for things to comment on in your partner just in order to escape repeating. The comment should only change when one of you notices the other doing something very definite.

However, you should also make sure that you notice and comment on significant things. Part of our real-life social training is the process of 'editing out' – choosing not to comment on certain things we observe in others, and even pretending to ourselves that we haven't observed them – but within this exercise *nothing is outside the frame*. If your partner stumbles on his words, shifts uneasily in his seat, starts speaking in a way that is false or contrived, or takes unnecessarily long pauses, you must notice, and comment on, all of these things. If you do not, then you will start to become *complicit* with your partner, by which I mean that you enter into an unspoken agreement not to embarrass him or make him uncomfortable. This may be all very considerate and may create a very safe relationship, but it will also quickly turn the exercise into a meaningless party game. Only by ruthlessly exposing everything you see, truthfully and with an unforced spontaneous reaction, can the repetition succeed.

Another thing to avoid is *doing things deliberately* in order to provoke a comment. This is both manipulative and evasive, because it tries to control your partner's responses and comments, and it keeps you in a state of self-consciousness, within which nothing spontaneous or unguarded can happen. You have to be brave enough to focus on the other actor and *let yourself alone*.

The last rule is that you have to keep the whole thing going. The repetition must always continue, even when you feel thrown or exposed. It is in those moments where you let go of control that we get the most truthful responses.

Example 1

So we start. Once again, what seemed like quite a slight adjustment to the exercise turns out to be a major change which the actors find quite challenging.

The first pair start off pretty much as before, and for quite a while the comment ('You've got spiky hair.') goes back and forth without change. It is as though they are still doing simple repetition. I can feel the rest of the group becoming restive. We are all wondering why neither actor is commenting on what they see.

When we stop and ask them, Actor 1 replies that he couldn't see anything to comment on, and it was certainly true that both actors, presumably because they were aware that their every move was open to scrutiny, had been sitting very still.

At this point, one of the group expresses the concern that the whole premise of Standard Repetition – to observe and comment on someone else's every action – is guaranteed to produce tension and a closed body. I agree that the danger is there, but point out to the group that what we have arrived at is the absolute crux of the actor's dilemma – does the actor reveal in the space only what has been painstakingly rehearsed, or can he train himself to be more human, more spontaneous, more real, by becoming comfortable with the experience of being watched?

*

This brings us back to first Meisner principles. Meisner Technique is based on the concept of 'the reality of doing'. You do not pretend to do something – you really do it. In this case, what you really do is to observe changes in your partner and respond to them. It is by doing this that you can allow the anxiety of being *watched* and the feeling of *performing* to be replaced by the fascination of the task and the need to fulfil it.

So what if there seems to be nothing there to observe? You are waiting for changes, yet your partner isn't moving a muscle. The answer is that *this fact itself is worthy of comment*. In real life, if you talk to someone and they remain completely blank, in terms of facial expression and body language, you will probably try to find out if they are okay, or if they have understood what you were saying. In the same way, if your Standard Repetition partner sits like a talking statue, then you can comment on it:

A1	You're not moving.
A2	I'm not moving.
A1	You're not moving.
A2	I'm not moving.
A1	You're completely still.
A2	I'm completely still.
A1	You're frozen.
A2	I'm frozen.

And so on. Once your partner realises that stillness is not an effective hiding place – that it is read and commented upon just like any other physical choice, he may give up trying to censor or minimise his physical language, and get on with the job of observing and responding.

Example 1 continued

Gradually, these two actors shift the attention away from themselves, and as their bodies start to relax, little inadvertent responses start to happen. We in the group see these responses, and we understand what within the relationship and dialogue stimulates them, which allows us to believe in their unself-conscious authenticity.

We also notice, however, that the actors themselves often seem to miss or ignore little physical changes in each other. Obviously, the physical vocabulary of an actor sitting on a chair is limited, but within that limitation there are many gestures and involuntary responses that can happen. Examples might be:

- Shifting on your seat
- Touching, stroking your leg
- Folding your arms
- Screwing up your face
- Squinting an eye
- Putting your head on one side
- Raising your eyebrows
- Shrugging your shoulders
- Licking your lips
- Twitching your foot

Many of these things happen, as the group can testify, in direct response to the dialogue, yet somehow both actors at various times seem to edit them out, almost as though they have previously trained themselves not to notice anything that is not consciously displayed for comment.

When questioned, actors often claim not to have noticed these responses in their partner. Sometimes they admit that they did observe them, but were unable to articulate what they saw quickly enough. My response to this in the group is that you need to use the Meisner work to train this level of responsiveness into yourself. Just as a doctor reads a patient's physical signs to discover the nature of a disorder, or a barrister reads a witness to detect inconsistencies and discomfort within a cross-examination, so you the actor will read another actor's reactive gestures in minute detail, as part of the process of learning to observe.

Most of you are already adept at reading others, but you often switch off your heightened sensors in everyday life, simply because they are not necessary, and would lead to your being overstimulated with huge amounts of surplus information about everyone you meet, from the person serving coffee to the person sitting opposite you on the train.

So you reserve the super-responsive mode for important or heightened situations, such as an audition, a date, or a street conflict. Within such contexts, you are utterly engaged. Your eyes, ears and bodies are fine-tuned to detect the minutest changes in others, and to alter your own behaviour on a moment-to-moment basis.

Of course, this hyper-attentiveness is usually brought about by situations in which you are acutely aware of the need to bring about one particular outcome and avoid another. This need might be about relationships, money or self-preservation, but in these situations you rarely have to make a conscious choice about whether or not to engage with the other person. Once you have understood the stakes, the rest is largely chemistry – the adrenalin pumping through your bloodstream does the job for you.

Having said that, many of the situations that engage you in this way are entered into voluntarily, and the stakes, though high in the moment, have no real consequence. There are many games, such as poker, whose outcome can depend on an accurate reading of a partner, or an ability to predict future moves.

These are not necessarily life-changing, but you invest in them because it is in your nature to do so. You use your imagination to raise the emotional stakes to a level where you can place all your attention, for the duration of the game, on a clearly perceived yet fictional objective. In the same way, you can learn to invest, not just in a play, but in a workshop exercise, so that you are always working with heightened awareness and maximum sensitivity to what is happening around you.

Through Standard Repetition, you can teach yourself to read another person and respond with a similarly high level of awareness. Little by little you can train yourself to leave nothing outside of the frame, to edit nothing out, and to articulate speedily and precisely what has been observed. Once you have seen the 'editing out' process in action while watching from the sidelines, you begin to understand your own evasion strategies, and after discussion you are equipped to observe and comment in a more searching and uncensored way.

Once you have started to 'include' everything that happens within your observational scope, you become a more honest actor, because you stop trying to deal with two different realities simultaneously. The habit of choosing to ignore what you see, and even to pretend you have seen something else, is quite deeply engrained in some actors, but however practised you are at deceiving yourselves and your audiences, this process will always ring false somewhere within you, and your audience will always pick that up.

Example 2

The next pair, Actors 3 and 4, enter the space with this in mind. The good news is that they are both so intent on observing every tiny change in one another that they forget to be self-conscious. The bad news is that the effort of trying to put their observations into words makes them stumble, hesitate and giggle.

At this point I decide to take the pressure off and give everyone time just to practise the skill of reading and responding. I pair everyone off, and free them from the spotlight. For a long time, up to an hour, they simply work the mental 'muscle sequence' which allows them to perceive, formulate and articulate without stumbling, giggling or judging. Most of them pass through these stages, and also through a period of boredom. Few achieve anything approaching real openness or intimacy, since the experience remains an unfamiliar and exposing one, but at least everyone learns the simple skill of seeing something and saying clearly and immediately what they have seen.

In the discussion that follows, one or two of you comment that you found it hard to stay engaged because you couldn't believe in the significance of the things you were commenting on. They seemed too small, too inconsequential, too unworthy of comment. I detect a longing for fictitious characters, stories, pithy dialogue, high drama.

I understand this need, but, should you feel this frustration in Meisner work, remind yourself that a momentary glance between two strangers at the bus stop can potentially be more compelling than the closing scenes of *Hamlet*, if you are genuinely engaged with each other in one but not the other. Drama can exist in the tiniest of moments, not just in monumental conflicts. As actors, you need to assume that there is a hidden life in everyone, which you can catch glimpses of but can probably never fathom. The little actions and gestures that you capture and comment on are tiny expressions of that hidden life, and they should whet your appetite for more discovery.

You also have to assume that even when you have been working with the same people over a long period of time and think you know them fairly well, there is still much that is hidden. The old expression 'familiarity breeds contempt' should not apply here. There is always more to know – if you can just allow yourselves to look.

Example 2 continued

So we start again, and this time there is a different atmosphere. It is as if the actors have become students of each other's behaviour. At first they are rather earnest and clinical in their comments, and as a result the comments, and the gestures that inspire them, become rather chopped up. After a few nudges, however, they relax and start to inflect the comments with a sense not just of what they see, but the context in which they see it. For example:

A3	You licked your lips. (*'I exposed you.'*)
A4	I licked my lips. (*'Yes, you exposed me.'*)
A3	You licked your lips. (*'I embarrassed you.'*)
A4	You grinned. (*'You think it's funny.'*)
A3	I grinned. (*'Yes I do.'*)
A4	You grinned. (*'You're not even ashamed.'*)
A3	I grinned. (*'No, I'm not.'*)
A4	You grinned. (*'You should be ashamed of yourself.'*)
A3	You narrowed your eyes. (*'You're cross.'*)
A4	I narrowed my eyes. (*'Yes, perhaps I am.'*)

The bits in the brackets are, of course, just my reading of the possible subtext within a short exchange, based on the vocal tones and body language of the actors. Had this subtext been contrived by the actors or imposed on the exchange, or had the physical gestures been manufactured, I would have challenged it, but this was clearly not the case. Each verbal or physical reaction emerged easily and spontaneously from the actors' observations of one another, and it was easy for all of us watching to see that this was so.

From this point, the group begins to understand how each physical response is part of the dialogue, and that nothing is insignificant, even if it does not arise directly out of the exchange. For instance, if Actor 3 sees Actor 4 scratch his ear, while it might just have been a random itch which prompted the gesture, Actor 3 may still interpret it in a way which Actor 4 can read and respond to. The subtext could be anything from 'You're more interested in your ear than in me,' to 'You can't sit still.' It could even be 'I don't know why you did that.'

After a while the actors also start to comment on the manner of each other's delivery. This is a natural and allowable development within the exercise. Comments such as 'You hesitated,' 'You stumbled on your words,' or 'You raised your voice,' make direct reference to what the actor hears as well as what she sees.

As this starts to happen, however, another issue arises. Thus far we have concentrated on how the actor observes and comments, but now we also have to look at how the actor *repeats*. What are we actually saying when we repeat?

In Simple Repetition, the comment, which never changes, is about a simple visual fact. The nature of the comment is in itself of little importance, and the actor who repeats it is unlikely to find it hard to speak, unless it is a personal comment such as 'You've got acne.' The meaning, in Simple Repetition, is derived almost entirely from the vocal choices and body language.

In Standard Repetition, this is also the case, but since the comment continually changes, there is a constant risk of being taken unawares by a comment that points out something you might not even have been aware of. 'You stroked your leg,' or 'You pursed your lips,' are examples of comments which, while not shocking in themselves, can make you feel exposed and uncomfortable.

Your habitual response to such feelings may be to operate defence mechanisms – to giggle, or to make your voice flat and expressionless, or to 'de-voice', cutting off the natural connection that the inhaled breath makes between head and body, thought and emotion.

It is important that you not only recognise such responses and the reasons for them, but actively seek to get past your defences, otherwise you can never achieve the level of unforced responsiveness that, for the actor, should be second nature.

By the time you have reached this stage of the work, you will have observed first hand the involuntary defence mechanisms at work. To watch someone blocking, however unconsciously, a connection and a response, is actually a deeply frustrating experience, because it is precisely that connection and the spontaneous interaction that make acting exciting to watch. Actors should be supportive and understanding of each other within this work, but at the same time you need to affirm clearly the truth of what you observe, and make a collective choice to help each other move forward.

The issue here, as you may discover when you analyse the work, is not the literal truth of the observation, but the subtext. You are all worried about judgement and interpretation. Comments such as 'You licked your lips,' or 'You stroked your leg,' might indicate a sensual involvement that you are embarrassed to acknowledge or have made public. It is all part of your desire to maintain control over the signals you give out, not to let any information escape without your conscious consent. Once you start to realise that not only are you transmitting significant amounts of information through body language and reactive gesture, but that your partner is no longer politely going to edit out the signals that might embarrass you, you feel intensely exposed.

It takes a real act of trust, and a real effort of will, to allow both your partner and the rest of the group to see what they see, to think what they think, without censorship or attempts to manipulate their experience. On a simple physical level, you have to lower your shoulders, relax your jaw, breathe into a released torso, and make a conscious effort to keep your body language open. On a more cerebral level, you have to make up your mind not to shrink from being observed. This decision is on a par with stripping off on a naturist beach, or opening your house to the public. There is an initial resistance, but there is also potentially a certain liberation in choosing to reveal rather than to conceal.

It can take you a while to make that decision and to be honest with yourself about carrying it through. Along the way there are certain tricks and manipulations which need to be exposed.

Example 2 continued

When we start the repetition again, it takes a while for the two actors to tune in to one another, but after a while they become very sensitised to the slightest change, and able to articulate what they see quickly and easily. At this stage, few of the comments present the actors with too much difficulty:

A3	You raised your right eyebrow.
A4	I raised my right eyebrow.
A3	You raised your right eyebrow.
A4	You raised your left eyebrow!
A3	I raised my left eyebrow!
A4	You raised your left eyebrow.
A3	You smiled.
A4	I smiled.
A3	You smiled.
A4	You stopped smiling.

A3   I stopped smiling.

A4   You grinned.

A3   I grinned.

A4   You grinned.

So far, so good. The observations are mostly about events that arise very predictably from the dialogue, and they come as no surprise, so the actors have no difficulty in accepting them. In fact, although the actors are working with less self-consciousness than before, their reactions, and therefore the comments, are still about the embarrassment and unfamiliarity they are experiencing. This is a stage you simply have to work through, sticking doggedly to the rules of the exercise until something slightly different happens. For example:

A3   You leaned forward.

A4   I leaned forward.

A3   You leaned forward.

A4   You leaned back.

A3   I leaned back.

A4   You bit your lip.

A3   I bit my lip.

A4   You bit your lip.

A3   I bit my lip.

A4   You did it again.

A3   I did it again.

A4   You did it again.

A3   You're swaying.

A4   I'm swaying.

A3   You were swaying.

A4   I was swaying.

A3	You stopped yourself.
A4	I stopped myself.
A3	You stopped yourself.
A4	I stopped myself.
A3	You backed off.
A4	I backed off.
A3	You backed off.
A4	You came forward.
A3	I came forward.

The observations are now clearly picking up both the conscious and the unconscious psycho-physical responses of each actor. In a case like this, however, it is likely that one actor will be processing differently from another because each is learning and progressing at a different rate.

In this case, Actor 4 is repeating the observations in a vulnerable yet open way – going on a journey in which he is making some choices, yet also accepting that he cannot always be in control.

Actor 3, by contrast, has adopted a 'sincere' tone of voice which has a certain resonance and emotional quality, but which is entirely within his control. The effect is that of watching a melodrama – beneath each line we can read some kind of emotionally charged subtext, but none of it is actually rooted in the moments and events of the relationship. It is as though Actor 3 has hidden his own true responses beneath an emotional 'wash'.

The group spots this immediately and challenges Actor 3, who, to his credit, accepts the observation, and admits that the group is right, although he claims not to have been entirely conscious of what he was doing. Actor 3 is keen to have another go, so we start again.

This time Actor 3 is a little bit passive, but after a while he begins to respond to the comments in a way that seems to be less manipulative and more spontaneous. However, in his efforts to be less in control and more vulnerable, he interprets every comment made about him as if it were a devastating wound and inflects his response accordingly. Little by little he becomes a victim, and it becomes clear that, although his responses are slightly more spontaneous than before, they are also way out of proportion to what is actually happening between him and his partner.

Meanwhile, Actor 4 is also engaged in a manipulation, partly stimulated by Actor 3. It is as though every comment made about him gives him a sort of dark masochistic pleasure. By overcompensating for his previous reserve, he has now gone beyond a simple openness into an 'attitude' of self-exposure. The overall effect is of a sexual power game played out between two participants in predetermined roles, rather like some of the role-playing in the earlier repetition sessions.

There is safety in playing 'attitudes' – you probably do it without thinking when you find yourself in unfamiliar environments. If you have watched plenty of theatre and television, you may be practised in the false art of playing fake emotional states, which are merely imitations of what you have seen other actors do. If you want to be a 'real' actor, you have to resist the temptation to limit the scope of your responses in this way. It seems a simple thing to ask, but to go against your most deeply ingrained social habits can feel like a violation of both your natural instincts and your sense of personal safety.

The means through which you control and manipulate your social responses is, of course, the breath. By regulating and restricting the flow of the breath into the body, tensing the ribs and stomach muscles at key moments, you can avoid the vulnerability that ensues when that which you are thinking, experiencing or expressing connects with your physical emotional centre. To remove your defences, therefore, you have to breathe differently.

It is often useful to think in terms of 'breathing in the other actor', as if your partner is radiating some invisible 'ether' which can only be understood by breathing it. This may sound very abstract, but actors often use imaginary ideas to stimulate changes in the way the body responds, and this is no different.

With perseverance, most actors can reach a new level with Standard Repetition. Actors who have experienced this report that they have genuinely 'been on a journey' together. The relationship changes and keeps changing. Neither actor gets stuck in one way of being, and the relationship itself does not get into a rut or go round in circles. There are moments of intimacy, moments of conflict, moments of vulnerability and moments of laughter. The actors do not dictate the journey – the journey simply happens.

I should stress at this point that to make discoveries and breakthroughs in repetition work is a careful and painstaking process, involving a lot of careful observation and comment from the group and the teacher. Like much of actor training, repetition requires you to stop, reflect and try again many times until the shifts you are looking for begin to happen. Some people will make big changes which are satisfying and encouraging for everyone, but for others the true benefits of the work will reveal themselves not in the Meisner classes themselves, but in rehearsal and performance at a later stage of training, or even professional life. What is taking place here is a kind of reprogramming of your patterns of response, and that inevitably takes time.

I can guarantee that, once you have begun to hear your group's observations and started to recognise and modify your own behaviours, the shift will start to happen.

5

Psychological Repetition

'A moment of silence
isn't a nothing'

Psychological Repetition

The name I give to this type of repetition is my own. As far as I know, Meisner himself did not distinguish it from Standard Repetition, and other Meisner practitioners I have worked with actually disapprove of it. My view is that it is an essential development on from Standard Repetition, and that, provided the actors are ready, it can form a major stepping stone in the journey towards story and character.

Psychological Repetition

For the most part, Psychological Repetition works in exactly the same way as Standard Repetition, and for much of the time *is* actually the same thing. The significant difference is that in Psychological Repetition *you are allowed to comment not just on literal, physical happenings, but on responses that you genuinely read within the other actor.* For the first time, comments such as 'That annoyed you,' 'You found that amusing,' 'That surprised you,' are allowed as part of the conversation. In other words, you are now able to observe, recognise and comment on the emotion itself, not just its outward manifestation.

You will notice that I avoid expressing the comment as 'You're annoyed,' 'You're amused,' or 'You're surprised,' for the same reason that I insisted that all comments in Standard Repetition be made in the past tense. To use the present tense implies an ongoing emotional state. While this may occasionally be the case, which means that we can't rule out present-tense comments, on the whole we are commenting on moments of reaction that have already happened.

You should not be allowed to progress from Standard to Psychological Repetition until you are ready, the reason being that Psychological Repetition can all too easily become a manipulative mind game if one or both of the participants are still either defensive or overtentative.

The most important rule about this type of repetition is that you *genuinely have to see* what you comment on. It must be clear and obvious, not an educated guess, and certainly not a wild guess. The benchmark here is that other people in the group observing must also be able to see whatever you are commenting on.

Those Meisner practitioners who frown on this kind of repetition most probably do so because they are worried that actors who have spent so long learning to have a genuine response to real happenings may relapse into a less honest practice, in which they more or less invent the other actor's thoughts and attitudes, and respond to their own conjecture rather than the reality of the situation. There is also a danger that actors may misuse the power that this exercise gives them, in order to embarrass or unsettle their partner, or make them laugh.

While admitting that these dangers exist, I contend that you cannot move the work on until you allow yourselves to be specific about what you read in your partner's face, body and gestures. Your aim, as students of Meisner Technique, must ultimately be to practise the skills of openness and responsiveness, which you have mastered in repetition exercises, within character, text and story, and to do this you need to start talking about feelings.

The power of Psychological Repetition is two-fold. To notice that someone has had a particular reaction, and comment on it directly, is an experience that can evoke a strong emotional response. To hear that about ourselves, and have to repeat it, can have an even more profound effect. Very often it is in this version of the exercise that the 'lid' starts to come off the actors' emotions.

At this level of repetition, actors are sometimes tempted to stray from the basic rule that all dialogue must be statements or repetitions of direct observations. Occasionally there are denials, questions, orders or self-observations that burst out quite spontaneously. You have to be rigorous in avoiding all of these, because on some level they are all defensive or controlling; in other words, the opposite of what repetition is about. At a much later stage you may be allowed to use some of these, but not yet.

By the time you start to do Psychological Repetition, you will need to have lost much of your self-consciousness. The giggling and the more blatant status games should anyway have disappeared, but as before, the introduction of a more complex and potentially more exposing version of the exercise will set you back a little. The first hour will probably see most of you revert to old habits – shallow breath, flat monotonous voices, and of course the loss of the fundamental objective, which was set up in the first exercise, and which you need in order to maintain energy and keep you on the front foot.

The leap into Psychological Repetition is possibly one of the biggest and hardest. The reason, as you quickly realise and articulate, is that in all previous versions, you were dealing with irrefutable facts. Some of these were revealing, but the rules of the exercise set limits within which you felt reasonably safe. With this version of the exercise, there are still rules, but you feel less safe, because someone is reading your 'inner' life as well as just commenting on its outward manifestations. This potentially gives your partner extraordinary power and makes you very vulnerable, although of course the reverse is also the case.

To reduce the element of exposure you can start with another preparatory exercise:

Psychological Repetition – Preparatory Exercise

Working once again in pairs (it is always good to work with as many different partners as possible), you all try out Psychological Repetition simultaneously, without the scrutiny of the group. After a few minutes, I start to circulate and observe what is happening.

Almost invariably the following things can be observed. Firstly, a number of rather generic comments, which arise over and over again. These include 'You're confused,' 'You're annoyed,' and 'You're upset.' The problem with these, quite apart from their lack of specificity, is that they are usually the result of guesswork as you try to read one another. I suspect that they are also 'projections' of your own feelings onto your partner. I remind you that you can still comment on concrete physical happenings, and that the 'psychological' comments should be reserved for those very obvious moments of change or reaction that you see in one another. I also advise you to find a way of phrasing the observation so that it is about a moment, not a continuous state.

You may also find that the repetition has turned entirely into a 'guess what I'm thinking' game, which is very intense and apparently intimate but entirely fake. You may also have lost the honesty you found in Standard Repetition, and the openness to moments of surprise and exposure.

Worse than this, you may find that you are deliberately manufacturing emotions for your partner to comment on. Without realising you are doing it, you may be pretending to have reactions such as shock at your partner's observations; and rather than seeing through the fake emotion, your partner probably goes along with it, commenting on what he is being shown rather than what he actually sees, so that the whole exercise becomes increasingly superficial and dishonest.

For me this reveals a disturbing truth about how a lot of actors understand emotion in the acting space, and I don't just mean actors in training. Within the world of television acting, many actors who have never learned to be emotionally available manage to signal emotion (sometimes quite skilfully) in a way that gives us a visual indicator of what we are supposed to be seeing, without actually offering it.

This is painful to watch, although we are so used to fake emotion that some of us have lost the ability to distinguish it from the real thing. But as actors and artists, you need constantly to be challenging fakeness both in yourselves and others. If you are to achieve truth and depth in your own acting, you have to retrain yourselves to expect and demand truth and depth from your peers.

From here the work becomes significantly more challenging, because now I am not just asking you to observe with a little more care and diligence – I am requiring that you shed layers of artifice from your own work and start to question those layers of artifice in others.

This is quite a struggle, because first of all you have to admit to yourself that you are both working superficially and allowing your peers to do the same. Secondly, you have to have the courage to say, 'You faked that response,' or something similar, within the exercise.

Once you have understood the need for honesty and detailed observation, things can start to change. Much of what you observe is not high drama, just simple thoughts captured in a gesture and expressed in a few words. An example might be:

A1   You clasped your hands.

A2   I clasped my hands.

A1   You sighed.

A2   I sighed.

A1   You sighed.

A2   I sighed.

A1   You're passive.

A2   I'm passive.

A1   You decided to stop being passive.

A2   I decided to stop being passive.

A1   You sat up.

A2   I sat up.

A1   You shook your head.

A2   I shook my head.

A1   You tried to shake yourself awake.

A2   I tried to shake myself awake.

A1   You tried to find something to comment on.

A2   I tried to find something to comment on.

A1   That embarrassed you...

A2   That embarrassed me... You found that amusing.

A1   I found that amusing.

A2   You found that very amusing.

This kind of observation may not be wildly dramatic, but you will at least be learning to observe quickly and truthfully, and to focus on real moments rather than performing a series of fake ones. Remember, there is always something to observe, even (or even especially) when your partner is clearly trying to give nothing away.

With the group watching you again, it can take a while for you to relax in to the repetition while remaining truthful and incisive. There may be an initial fear of 'imposing' responses, or being caught 'faking', which leads in the first instance to a fixed and inhuman way of working. I often have to remind actors to breathe, and to see the exercise as the development of a relationship rather than the execution of a task.

Once you have stopped worrying about getting the exercise wrong, and started to be absorbed by your partner, another deeper fear sets in, which is that of being exposed or having to expose someone else. All too often actors who have achieved a degree of responsiveness in earlier versions of repetition find that this exercise takes them outside their comfort zones. The examples below seek to illustrate some of the reactions you might have to Psychological Repetition, and how you might deal with them.

Example 1

Two actors start the exercise from a place of mistrust, as if expecting the worst. Actor 1 has a fixed and nervous smile; Actor 2 has a slightly brittle, tense manner. Both are clearly frightened and trying not to show it.

To begin with, the repetition goes nowhere. They repeat dutifully and for the most part within the rules of the exercise, but neither is prepared to be affected, and neither is genuinely open to change. They seem unwilling or unable to commit either to their comments or their repetitions, yet neither is prepared to acknowledge this within the comments. Far from revelling in the intimacy of the relationship, they seem uncomfortable and reticent.

*

To address this discomfort you might start by considering analogies of situations where openness and generosity are built into the encounter, such as counselling sessions – although of course within this exercise there are no predetermined roles. As I am at pains to clarify, it is not that I want you to work like counsellors or like their clients, but I do want you to start to become more at ease within situations which may evoke unfamiliar or even disturbing feelings. Repetition at any level, but particularly at this level, can often bypass defences in a most unexpected way, but only if your attitude towards it is one of courage and a desire to explore and discover.

Example 1 continued

When the actors in my example start again, Actor 2 (the brittle one) makes a real effort to open up, to breathe, and to focus his attention on the other actor. The result is that, almost from the first, he starts to feel a deep emotion, and soon he is speaking through tears. I remind him, without stopping the exercise, that he needs to work *from* and *through* the emotion, and he keeps the repetition going.

A1	You're crying.
A2	I'm crying.
A1	You're crying.
A2	You're concerned.
A1	I'm concerned.
A2	It's made you uncomfortable.
A1	It's made me uncomfortable.
A2	You want me to stop.
A1	I want you to stop.

A2   You want me to stop.

A1   You can't stop.

A2   I can't stop.

A1   You wiped your eyes.

A2   I wiped my eyes.

Actor 1 is moved and concerned, and completely forgets his own fears. He experiences a strong, reciprocal opening-up, at least for the time being. Eventually, Actor 2 works through his emotion and once again turns his attention to his partner. Actor 1 has been happy with the previous transaction, which kept the focus off him. He is less happy with the new transaction, in which his partner, now emotionally open and resonant, is starting to observe him in a much more searching way. The fixed smile and the closed body return.

On some level, this is a truthful response, since it arises genuinely from Actor 1's observation of his partner. The repetition exercises, though, are designed expressly to prevent actors retreating behind their habitual defences whenever they feel vulnerable. I remind Actor 1 that his task is to continue to observe his partner, *not* to watch his partner observing him! Gradually, by turning his full attention back on to Actor 2, Actor 1's body opens and the smile disappears.

A large part of Meisner training is making yourself follow its rules, which are clear and simple. When you find yourself becoming tense, shallow-breathing and ceasing to be responsive, it is almost always because you have allowed the focus to shift back on to you rather than keeping it on the other person. It may feel odd, but you can, by an effort of will, get that focus back on to your partner. The task of reading and commenting is actually a simple and literal one, which can help you out of your self-consciousness and into a more relaxed and open state.

When you are nervous or fearful it is always helpful to have something simple and concrete to do.

Example 2

Actor 3 is habitually closed and suspicious. His habit is to scrutinise others through half-closed eyes, and when he speaks he always does so in the manner of someone who is testing the water rather than allowing himself to make a clear and spontaneous statement. He lingers on vowel sounds as if reluctant to commit to a statement and let it go. By contrast, Actor 4 is open and determined to make Actor 3 open up. Predictably, the exercise quickly becomes a game of pursuit, in which Actor 4 tries to get Actor 3 to respond to him, while Actor 3 adopts a low-energy nasal monotone whose continuing subtext is 'You won't get past me'.

Once again I get the sense of agendas and roles that exist in the actors' own lives and relationships, being played out in the acting space and imposing restrictions on the journey these two can go on together.

As I mentioned at the start of this book, Meisner work as I teach it does not take place in a vacuum, but within an overarching training process and philosophy, into which this work is embedded. It is invariably at the beginning of the second year of full-time training that I start Meisner repetition with acting students. This is because it is the point at which one can say to the actors, 'This is what acting asks of you – do you really want to do this?', because at this point they have the physical and vocal tools to choose to be actors if that is what they really want.

Every actor responds differently to Meisner, but sooner or later the exercises start to expose the limitations you have placed upon yourself. Put simply, you start to see just how much you are not prepared to give up in the pursuit of your craft, in terms of personal risk. This is not a physical risk, but the risk of being seen, exposed, judged, and, beyond that, of having to experience uncomfortable emotions.

If you habitually work defensively I will ask you: 'Why are you doing this?' There can be only a few possible answers. The first is that you are willing but scared, which is understandable. In this case, the way forward is for you to keep doing the exercises and keep trying to apply the basic rules and principles with a variety of partners until you start to feel less scared and more exhilarated.

It may be that deep down you don't really believe that an actor needs to work with that much openness or to give up control to other actors in this way. It is true that while some actors who come to drama school see it as a life-changing journey, others consciously or unconsciously resist change, perhaps believing they can be selective within the training, taking on board some aspects while dodging others. Again, it is not that I don't understand why and how those feelings are present; however, unless you deal with them, you can't really move forward, and you can't really be an actor.

This is the stage of the work in which I would normally let you know, reasonably firmly, that it is no longer acceptable for you to return to square one every time a new and slightly more challenging form of repetition is introduced. It is now up to you to ensure that both you and your peers are working to the rules, genuinely exploring, because that is what actors do.

Example 2 continued

Actor 3 listens both to me and to the group, and takes everything on board. He stops being watchful and suspicious, and starts seeing his partner as an object of interest, the site of something potentially significant to him. In doing so, he becomes much less defensive, and in the face of Actor 4, who is a very compassionate and unashamedly emotional character anyway, he quickly becomes emotional.

Instead of *allowing* the emotion, he quickly suppresses it, but does persist with the exercise. However, Actor 4, who has observed his reaction and his successful attempts to stifle it, feels responsible and culpable, and is therefore unable to verbalise what he sees. He continues to observe and comment, but because he has ignored the most important event, his comments ring slightly false, and the relationship starts to plateau.

This is another very common occurrence – a reluctance among actors to affect one another emotionally, even in the fictional space, or in this case also with a sense of guilt when they do. Again this is a truthful reaction, but its effect is to shut down and obscure the more important truth, namely what it was you observed in your partner within that moment.

It may be useful at this point to stop and talk about what it is you saw but were unable – at the time – to speak about. Sometimes the group can help you by articulating what they saw and offering you the words you need. By finding a way of describing an event, such as 'You stifled your emotion,' or 'You censored yourself,' you can become used to working with an unfamiliar vocabulary. To have ownership of that vocabulary is highly empowering, because it gives you not only a means of expression, but also permission to notice things and articulate them without guilt.

Actor 4's problem is not that he is unable to see, nor even that he doesn't ultimately have the words to express what he sees, but a lack of connectedness between what he observes and what he allows himself to comment on. Self-censorship is part of your social training, but even in your early adulthood it is so embedded that you have to train yourself to respond differently.

Example 2 continued

By gradually acquiring both the vocabulary and the permission to comment on exactly what he sees, Actor 4 becomes bolder. He starts with a slightly inarticulate honesty, in which he struggles for the right words, but eventually he is able to comment with more clarity and conviction:

A4   You shrugged your shoulders.

A3   (*Slightly startled.*) I shrugged my shoulders.

A4   You didn't know you did.

A3   I didn't know I did.

A4   You tensed your shoulders.

A3   I tensed my shoulders – you did the same.

A4   I did the same – that amused you!

A3   That amused me.

A4   That amused you.

A3   You didn't like me being amused.

A4   I didn't like you being amused.

A3   You thought I was laughing at you.

A4   I thought you were laughing at me.

A3   That wobbled you.

A4   That wobbled me – you think that's weird.

A3   I do think that's weird.

A4   You smiled but you're worried.

A3   I smiled but I'm worried.

A4   You said that mechanically.

A3   I said that mechanically.

A4   You didn't want to admit it.

A3   (*Slightly emotional.*) I didn't want to admit it.

*

From this fragment of dialogue, you can see that the more honest you become, the more effective and truthful the exchange. The art lies in training yourself to see and comment on the little concealments, moments of censorship and defence mechanisms your partner employs, while trying to remain open and accepting yourself.

Example 3

In the next pair of actors, Actor 5 is studiously non-confrontational – his habit is always to retreat from anything potentially difficult or adversarial. His strategy is to stop breathing and articulating when he receives any comment – he becomes passive, and his replies neutral, robotic. By contrast, Actor 6 is a 'power player'. His strategy is to be a commenter rather than a receiver, and he quickly falls into a habit of 'choosing to see' rather than actually seeing. His default statement is 'You're angry,' or 'You're annoyed,' which has the effect of putting his partner (I nearly said 'opponent') into a state of confusion while he remains in a position of power. His intonations and manner are those of a teacher addressing a slightly slow student. He also consistently misses what is actually happening in front of him and sees what he wants to see.

When challenged, Actor 6 is huffy and defensive. He persists in claiming that he is commenting on what he sees in Actor 5, and that he is doing so as honestly as he can. Actor 5 by contrast is bewildered by the comments, which don't accord at all with how he is actually feeling. At this point, one of the group raises a pertinent question. What happens if your partner makes a comment that you simply don't believe to be true, such as 'You're angry,' when you don't feel that at all? How can you honestly repeat something back which, for you, is false?

There are actually several ways in which you can deal with this situation without compromising your own honesty. If you feel that your partner has genuinely seen something in you, even if you weren't aware of it yourself, there may be a liberation in simply admitting it. However, if you are convinced they are attempting to manipulate you, you can repeat in a way which questions the statement, e.g.:

A1   (*Manipulation or misinterpretation.*) You're getting annoyed.

A2   (*Disbelief.*) I'm getting annoyed!?

A1   (*Genuine observation.*) You're getting annoyed.

A2   (*Acceptance.*) I'm getting annoyed now!

Or you can make the simple counter-statement 'You didn't see that,' which breaks the rule that you have to repeat the comment at least once, and should therefore be used sparingly or where you are absolutely convinced that your partner is deliberately imposing. Again, you have to have seen the manipulation taking place for this comment to be allowable.

It is important that neither of the last two options is used defensively, or to brush off a true observation. Here, as always, we rely on the group to be objective observers and to challenge evasive tactics.

Example 3 continued

The problem with Actor 6, it turns out, is that he is very unused to reading responses in others in a specific way, and still less accustomed to allowing the feelings of others to affect him. He doesn't like to be seen to flounder, though, so he engages in a series of confident guesses, which are wide of the mark but maintain him in a position of dominance. His demeanour and accent are convincing, but the group soon spots the fact that he is playing power games.

Once we have got through this, partly through the group's well-observed comments, Actor 6 is at a loss. He genuinely doesn't know how to proceed. I suggest to him that he returns to the literal comments of Standard Repetition, and only comments on Actor 5's feelings if he sees something very definite and unequivocal.

This works very well, because Actor 6, while maintaining his focus on Actor 5, is now able to observe with more honesty. The pressure to describe accurately Actor 5's reactions is removed, and most of the comments in that direction are now about physical gestures. This gives Actor 5 the space to comment back. Actor 6 is taken aback at first by some of the readings of him, and to begin with he uses the 'questioning' tactic to challenge the comments:

A5	You sat back in your chair.
A6	I sat back in my chair.
A5	You sneered.
A6	I sneered?
A5	You sneered.
A6	I sneered??
A5	You can't accept that.
A6	I can't accept that.
A5	You think I'm wrong.
A6	I think you're wrong.
A5	You said that aggressively.
A6	I said that aggressively.
A5	You said that aggressively.

A6   You didn't like that.

A5   I didn't like that.

It turns out that Actor 5 is quite observant and articulate, and quite often hits the nail on the head. Actor 6 tries hard not to be defensive or to brush comments away, and after a while begins to understand how it feels to admit something, not defensively, but as a simple acceptance of what someone else has seen. To hear a comment of this kind, to breathe and to repeat it back without either challenging it or disconnecting oneself from the statement, may seem a very simple thing to do, but it is actually quite difficult, as the group quickly discovers.

We have to stop several more times. The first time it is because Actor 6, having learned how to repeat with acceptance and understanding, starts to play low-status and humility, which may be in contrast to the previous power games, but is still in itself a safe choice, because it pre-empts and therefore precludes any genuine emotional response. By this time I hardly have to speak, because the group has become so articulate in feeding back to participants. Patiently, the group explains to Actor 6 that he needs to allow each moment to happen, rather than anticipating it or attempting to steer the direction of the relationship.

At this point, Actor 6 has a minor outburst. He claims that he doesn't understand what the group is talking about, and if he did he wouldn't know how to change it. He is very annoyed, but the annoyance clearly reveals his frustration at not being able to do the exercise 'well'. He is a person who wants to shine, and if possible to do so effortlessly, and to be engaged in a struggle of this kind feels very uncomfortable.

I intervene to point out to Actor 6 that his reaction to the group, together with the underlying emotion, is entirely believable. His vulnerability manifests itself through anger rather than distress, but the distress is still very evident, and is a direct response to observations the group has made about him. We do not for a moment doubt the genuineness of what he is feeling. The difference is that the group's observations take place within the 'real' world of the drama school and in the context of a collective aspiration to do well, in which Actor 6 has a major investment. By contrast, his partner's observations take place within the fictional world of the exercise, and Actor 6 is able to choose whether or not to see them as significant.

In Meisner you will inevitably experience the gap between the emotional energy you are prepared to expend in your own life, and that which you make available to your work. Once again it all comes back to the other actor and how you choose to see him. I believe that you *can* choose to ignore or shut out the presence of another actor, in the same way that you shut out the people you encounter on the bus, but you can also, if you wish, sensitise yourself to that presence – the choice is yours. If you genuinely want to be an actor, and to do what actors do, then you have to make the choice to experience the presence of other actors on an emotional and visceral level – to switch on that sensitivity you have previously reserved for your most intimate moments. Stanislavsky called this 'communion', and described it as an 'uninterrupted exchange of feelings, thoughts and actions' between actors.

Example 3 continued

It is at this point that Actor 6 really begins to understand what is required of him. Because he is, in this moment, still quite emotional, he is able to listen and absorb what is said on a different and more visceral level. Instead of striving to shut down, to recover himself and to resume his habitual stance, he stays open, and on the resumption of the exercise goes on a genuine and unforced journey.

When we stop again, it is Actor 5 we are looking at. His powers of observation and comment we have no problem with, but when the attention shifts onto him it is still painfully clear how physically uncomfortable he is both with hearing comments about himself (even simple physical facts) and with repeating them. The group notes that his body becomes limp and unresponsive, his voice becomes dull and his speech under-articulated. He appears like someone sunk into depression, unreachable.

When we point this out, he receives the information glumly and with resignation – this is a problem he is all too aware of but is unable to resolve. The very mention of it seems to push him further into despondency. I suggest to him that he should try to stop seeing the exercise as being in two parts – the part where he comments on Actor 6 and the part where Actor 6 comments on him – and start to see both as comments on their relationship. In other words, Actor 6 is not making defining statements about Actor 5 as a person – he is merely commenting on how Actor 5 is responding to him in that moment. And since every response is stimulated by the previous response, *each actor is always jointly responsible for everything which happens.*

I also remind Actor 6 that the relationship within a Psychological Repetition exercise should be both compassionate and exacting, and that comments can and should be made within the context of the underlying objective, which is to gain a deeper understanding of your partner.

This pair now begin their final attempt. They don't entirely succeed in overcoming the problems, and their work does still have a stop-start quality. But within it there are moments and sequences of openness, truthfulness and complete engagement, which they have not been able to reach before.

A5   You scrutinised me.

A6   I scrutinised you.

A5   You were trying to work something out.

A6   I was trying to work something out.

A5   You were trying to work something out.

A6   I was trying to work something out.

A5   You wanted to see inside me.

A6   You didn't see that.

A5   I didn't see that.

A6   You agreed.

A5   I agreed.

A6   You sat back.

A5   I sat back.

A6   Your body's tense.

A5   My body's tense.

A6   You don't like being looked at.

A5   I don't like being looked at.

A6   You closed your body.

A5   I closed my body.

A6   You closed your body.

A5   You criticised me.

A6   I criticised you.

If you really abide by the rules of this Psychological Repetition, it won't be false and it won't just descend into a superficial game, because, provided you are really watching, and provided you are not prepared to play along with your partner's manipulations and evasions, there is always something real to observe, even if it is not what your partner wanted you to see.

Once you have understood this, your response should be to raise the stakes within this exercise and be ruthless in 'seeking and destroying' each other's strategies for avoiding real connection and keeping a partner at arm's length. Any group embarking on Psychological Repetition will quickly identify within its individuals a certain level of fear and defensiveness, and a desire to maintain control within the exercise, which is detrimental to the training aims. The prevailing feeling within your group will often be the determining factor in how quickly the work proceeds.

Key to achieving this is the principle that, rather than being responsible for taking down your own barriers (which would be very difficult), you can instead become responsible for removing your partner's barriers, and vice versa. To do this you will need to sign up to a new kind of group relationship. As we have seen in the examples, many individuals within a group can be reluctant to challenge one another or to question each other's integrity within the work. To do so would be to upset the delicate balance of the group culture, which is to avoid open criticism and to observe the hidden pecking order and power structures.

For you to progress through this stage of your training, this culture has to change. You need to become secure with a group rigour, and you need to feel safe receiving positive and supportive criticism. Only by setting up within your group a new individual and collective work ethic can you hope to develop craft and embed good practice within your professional skillbase. Meisner work can be a positive mechanism for making that cultural change, because it is so structured that actors usually feel safe enough to take increasing risks.

One of the key features of this version of the exercise is that, to an even greater extent than before, you become responsible for your partner's behaviour, and vice versa. Hence if you are using unconscious strategies for keeping your partner at a metaphorical arm's length, you don't have to worry about this (worrying about yourself is always debilitating within a Meisner exercise), because it is your partner's job to identify your strategies and to challenge you. So your objective is always centred within them, and theirs within you.

Little by little, if you stick to the rules and listen to those observing you, you will start to 'nail' each other – tentatively at first, then with increasing confidence. Try to resist old habits, such as every now and then 'checking in' with your partner, either through a smile or through a brief pause, as if to say 'It's not real, is it?' Meisner work cannot be about complicity, because this lets you off the hook and pushes you further from achieving the objective. As I keep reminding you, nothing is outside the frame, so any attempt to suggest an 'alternative' safe reality, in which everything is the same as it always was, and this is 'just a game', should be challenged within that frame, not played along with. The same rule will ultimately have to apply to the actors' work on text and in character.

6

Objectives
and Activities

'Everything is based on life,
on reality'

Objectives and Activities

Before embarking on the next stage of Meisner work, in which you finally get up from the chairs and become physically active, you will need to spend at least an hour with one partner in unobserved and uninterrupted Psychological Repetition, immersing yourself in the world of that relationship and its parameters, as well as strengthening your new-found capacity for clear and honest observation.

For the first ten minutes or so you may find it possible to keep at least partly emotionally and mentally detached from the other actor. After half an hour, the world of the exercise will probably begin to take over, and by the time you stop, after a full hour, you will most likely have forgotten everything else. Quite apart from anything else this is a reminder to you that a deeper level of engagement with a role and with a fictional world is entirely within your grasp – you only have to want it.

It may take most of the hour before you genuinely begin to drop your defences, stop playing games and start to be 'real'. You may find that you will experience moments of real connection and responsiveness only during the last five minutes.

Before that point is reached, you may become frustrated or bored, and feel tempted to give up and walk away. Yet the point at which you take a deep breath and decide to carry on may be the moment that you truly break down the barrier between *your real feelings* and *the feelings you think you should be having*.

As actors, you probably suffer from constant anxiety about your ability to feel the right emotion at the right point. You may lack faith in your own emotional resources, and you may mistakenly understand emotion as something that can be turned on and off from within like a tap. This may lead you to develop techniques for acting emotion that have little to do with either your thoughts or your own emotional rhythms.

The danger here is that your emotional vocabulary as an actor may develop at a distance from your real inner life, and the two may be unable to meet. During a Meisner exercise, particularly within the early sessions, you can often see clear evidence of the separation between your feelings *about* the exercises – which are clear, strong and passionate – and your feelings *within* the exercises – which to begin with are often trapped or stifled. What you need to realise is that this boundary is largely a spurious one. In the moment of doing, there is no 'real' you and 'fictional' you – there is only the single reality of the moment.

With this in mind, you can begin the next stage of the Meisner work, which is about using repetition within a series of more dynamic physical contexts. Up to this point, all your repetition exercises have been 'chair-based', offering relatively little scope for the development of the physical/spatial relationship, and none for any physical contact. The next few exercises are designed to add a strong physical dimension to the mix, so that you can become accustomed not just to letting your responses be felt in the body, but to allowing – and following through – stronger and more active physical impulses.

The 'Walk Away' Exercise

You start with a very simple extension of the physical permissions of the seated exercise. Once again, you do Psychological Repetition over a relatively long period (up to an hour). This time, you have an additional option – before the exercise starts, additional pairs of empty chairs are placed around the space. You are then informed that if you reach a point within the hour where you become so frustrated, disappointed, annoyed or otherwise unable to continue, you have the option of getting up and walking to another space. Your partner then has to follow, and the repetition begins again but with an altered dynamic. This could potentially happen several times during the hour.

To use this option manipulatively, complicitly or as compensation for real commitment to the exercise is, of course, not allowed. Changing spaces must be a genuine response to the relationship, and not a way of injecting drama into an otherwise lifeless process. The impulse to move away must arise from the intensity of the relationship rather than a unilateral 'opting out' or imposed theatricality.

It is likely that very few of you will actually take the option to move. However, this new permission within the exercise should create an awareness that you and your partner cannot take each other for granted. The danger that your partner may suddenly abandon you can have the effect of lifting the level of physical energy as your ownership of the relationship – and a more active desire to avoid being left or being forced to leave – manifest themselves in your voice and body. It is a small but significant step towards making repetition more physical.

You may find that once you start the repetition, you quickly forget about the new permission – or rather you allow it to sit in the background of your awareness for the very valid reason that you are concentrating on the moment of doing. This is fine and normal! We cannot *play* given circumstances – we can only allow them to be present!

The next exercise quite deliberately takes you to the opposite end of the physical scale. Unlike all the previous exercises, it is played out in an arena of maximum physical contact and physical conflict. The idea is that, in the transition from chairs to space, the body does not get 'stuck' or confused, but is forced from the first moment to respond on a very basic level to its immediate circumstances. This is not a classic Meisner exercise, but it still follows the rules of repetition:

The Obstruction Exercise

This exercise offers actors a strong physical objective and obstacle through which you can continue to practise repetition. The extreme physical nature of this objective keeps the breath in the body and allows for a continuity and interplay between verbal and physical responses. For the first time you will be able to experience a direct relationship between observation, repetition and physical impulse.

You all pair off, and within each pair, decide who is the A and who the B. All the Bs go to the other side of the studio and talk amongst themselves, while I give the As a clear and strong task in the form of an ongoing objective.

The As are told that, when the repetition begins again, it will be without chairs, so that they and their respective B will be free to move within (although not out of) the space. The As are told that throughout the repetition exercise they must seek to *obstruct* their B, physically, firmly, using all their strength, but without aggression. In other words, anything

B tries to do, including sitting or standing still, must be physically and implacably opposed. The only thing A will allow B to do is speak – i.e. 'do' repetition. The repetition continues throughout.

Sending the As away, I now brief the Bs. They are told that they must *gain the respect* of their A. Again, this is an ongoing objective, but psychological and emotional rather than physical, and of course it will be played out in the context of the A's objective.

You also need to consider that, within this version of repetition (and indeed all those that follow), it will not always be possible for you to maintain visual contact with your partner. This means that to some extent your observations will now have to derive from the physical relationship with your partner or from other senses. For example, if she is pinning you to the floor, then even if you can't see her, you can say 'You're pinning me down'; or, if you can hear from her breathing that she is out of breath, then that too can be commented upon.

Unlike the 'Walk Away' Exercise, the Obstruction Exercise is always played out by individual pairs in front of the whole group.

The function of the repetition in this exercise is to maintain a sense of conversation and human connection within a physical/visceral struggle. The need to constantly comment and repeat ensures that you and your partner keep breathing and retain an awareness of each other's mental and emotional journey. The need to name your partner's reactions, moment by moment, within the context of the physical relationship and the pursuit of your own objective, maximises the emotional intensity. There is also so much going on within the verbal and physical interaction that there is almost no space for you to stand outside the action and comment, so you can achieve 'total immersion' in the exercise.

The move from sitting on chairs to such extreme physicality can present problems for some actors. I have listed below a series of potential pitfalls and problems which can occur within this transition. The diagnostic role of the group here is crucial. As in previous exercises, the group must exercise its own skills of observation and comment to identify and expose the problems, pointing out where the actors are going wrong and insisting that they work differently.

1. The A is too tentative
Just as you shied away from overstepping social boundaries in Psychological Repetition, so you may find it difficult to perform the task of the A with full commitment. What you have to understand is that this is *total* obstruction of anything the B tries to do. If the B wants to sit he must be yanked to his feet. If he wants to stand still he must be moved. If he wants to look at you his head must be turned away. If the A is smaller or weaker than the B then she simply has to try as hard as she can, rather than assuming that she can't succeed and giving up.

All too many As begin the exercise in a slightly half-hearted or apologetic way, and this reveals some wider issues about how trainee actors understand objectives. For an objective to be real you have to buy in to it emotionally – to understand the need or desire from which the objective derives, and to give yourself complete permission to pursue the objective with every ounce of your strength and power. In this case, you have to find your desire to repress and control – not a very pleasant quality, but one that everyone can relate to on some level. Within the permission of the exercise, you can pursue this ruthlessly and relentlessly. What you will also find is that the objective is self-perpetuating, since the moment you experience opposition and resistance in your partner, your body will automatically find a deeper commitment as the adrenalin kicks in.

2. The B becomes passive

Some people have an automatic 'shutdown', which kicks in when they face physical coercion. They become limp, weary and detached, as if to say, 'Do what you want to me, I don't care.' If you catch yourself doing this, you have to remind yourself that no actor can afford to remain in a safe and passive place. There is always an objective, and there is always a cost to achieving it. In this case, the rules of the exercise state that you want something from your A – i.e. respect. You should allow yourself to feel the lack of this respect within the journey of the exercise, and to respond accordingly.

The physical feeling of being restricted and controlled is inescapable, but most of us are able to limit our emotional response to such treatment. Here, though, you not only have a clear objective, you also have a task to continue observing and repeating as part of the quest to achieve that objective. To want something is to be active and therefore vulnerable – passivity is not an option within the terms of the exercise.

When you commit to your objective, you start to have a clear emotional sense of the gap between what your circumstances actually are and what you would like them to be. It is within that gap that the repetition takes place.

3. The A starts to annoy rather than obstruct

Sometimes the A backs away from the sheer physical demand of obstructing her partner, choosing instead to needle or annoy him. This is problematic because the level of emotional commitment needed to annoy someone is much lower than that required to obstruct and control them. It is important to identify this and get the A back on task.

Provided that your group is implacable in its insistence on the rules of the exercise, it can achieve a new level of investment from everyone fairly quickly, which will manifest itself in the repetition statements. It may take pressure from the group, but once you have bought in to the objectives and made a strong physical and emotional commitment to what you are doing, the dialogues can start to be intense and utterly absorbing, as in the following example:

Example 1

B	(*Growing frustration.*) You're holding my head.
A	(*Grim determination.*) I'm holding your head.
B	(*Realising what she's up against.*) You want to stop me moving.
A	(*Satisfaction at being able to express his objective so directly.*) I want to stop you moving.
B	(*Almost tearful.*) You're hurting me.
A	(*Scolding her.*) I'm hurting you... You're resisting.
B	(*Wrenching herself free.*) I'm resisting!
A	(*Annoyed, trying to take hold again.*) You broke free.
B	(*Triumphant, avoiding him.*) I broke free!
A	(*Grim, closing in on her.*) You broke free.
B	(*Alarmed.*) You're trying to hold me again!
A	(*Predator.*) I'm trying to hold you again.
B	(*Slightly hysterical.*) You're stopping me moving!
A	(*Calm, powerful.*) I'm stopping you moving.
B	(*Beside herself.*) You're a fucking arsehole!!

A   (*Brutal.*) Yes, I'm a fucking arsehole. You're very angry.

B   I'm very angry!

This example shows how the inescapable physical reality of this situation, if connected both to the dialogue and to a strong personal commitment to the objective, can take you on to a new level of involvement in repetition work. The repetition here is crucial, because it forces you to work simultaneously both physically/viscerally and intellectually/verbally, and to interweave these two into a single relationship or journey.

The dialogue above is fairly straightforward, since it is based on a familiar scenario of a strong person controlling a weaker through superior physical strength. Where the A is actually physically weaker than the B, different and more complex relationships can evolve, as in the following example:

Example 2

B   You're trying to turn my head away.

A   I'm trying to turn your head away... You won't let me.

B   I won't let you.

A   You're holding my wrists.

B   I'm holding your wrists.

A   You're holding my wrists.

B   I'm holding your wrists.

A   You're holding me away from you!

B   I'm holding you away from me.

A   You're holding me away from you.

B   You relaxed.

A	I relaxed.
B	You relaxed.
A	I relaxed.
B	You're waiting.
A	I'm waiting.
B	You're waiting for me to let you go.
A	I'm waiting for you to let me go.
B	You're waiting for me to let you go.
A	You don't trust me.
B	I don't trust you.
A	You don't trust me.
B	I don't trust you.
A	But you let me go.
B	I let you go.
A	You let me go.
B	You're trying to grab me again.
A	I'm trying to grab you again... You're backing away.
B	I'm backing away.
A	You don't want me to touch you.
B	I don't want you to touch me.
A	You're trying to stop me touching you.
B	I'm trying to stop you touching me.
A	You don't want me to be in control.
B	I don't want you to be in control.
A	You're scared.
B	I'm scared!!?
A	You're scared.
B	You're wrong.

A   I'm wrong... You stopped.

B   I stopped.

A   You're letting me touch you.

B   I'm letting you touch me.

A   You're letting me touch you.

Here the relationship starts off almost as a light-hearted physical game. What the repetition does is to introduce, fairly early on, a psychological power game, which counterpoints the unequal physical struggle. Without even knowing B's objective, A quickly observes B's discomfort in the face of all attempts to obstruct him, and B's consequent desire to keep A away from him. A then confronts him with this as a way of circumventing his physical strength. B, on the other hand, realises that to gain A's respect he must overcome his fear of control and have the courage to let A do what he likes.

The key to success in the Obstruction Exercise is courage. Not only do you have to bring all of your new-found skills of honesty and ruthless observation to the physical space, but you have to allow the group to see you committing, resisting or giving in to acts of genuine cruelty and repression. One of the hardest things about improvisation of any kind is that you, the actor, have to take responsibility for everything you do. There is no playwright to blame and no script telling you how to behave. You may fear the judgement of your peers, worrying that if you offer total commitment to the task they may be so convinced by it that they will assume they have somehow glimpsed the 'real' you. Your group may need to talk about these things, establishing a clear and mutual agreement that, within the margins of safety, anything and everything is acceptable.

As in previous exercises, the role of the group is to observe and comment. If the group sees you working tentatively, or if your body language signals apology, or if you smile in order to lessen the impact of what you are doing, the group can point this out. By placing a demand upon you, the group does not merely give you permission to commit to what the task demands – it actually insists upon it.

My hope is that by the time you have experienced the Obstruction Exercise, you will have understood first-hand what it means to genuinely use repetition to pursue an objective in the face of clear psycho-physical obstacles centred in the other person, and that you will see this as the basis of your work rather than any desire to perform or write a good story.

We now move on to the Objective and Activity Exercise. The main difference between this and the Obstruction Exercise is that here not only is it theoretically possible to achieve one's objective within the improvisation, but that failure or success is largely dependent on the way in which the relationship develops; the need to observe and read the other actor acutely is paramount.

The Objective and Activity Exercise

In this exercise, A has a strong objective centred in B, while B has a continuous task which has nothing to do with A – in other words, a slightly weaker objective to continue with the task. For example:

- A wants B to say he is beautiful.
- B has twenty chairs, neatly stacked. His task is to create a shape with the chairs, then to stack them again, then to create a new shape, and so on, continuously.

A Meisner teacher choosing objectives and activities for a group does not have to use the examples quoted in this chapter – the possibilities are endless. However, the following rules are best observed:

- The objective should be something clear and tangible that A wants B to do.
- The activity must be something that can be simply and easily done in the space, and is an open-ended activity – i.e. it will not be completed within the duration of the exercise.

A, who has the stronger objective, must pursue it at all times. B is told she can pause the activity in order to engage with A, but only if she feels it necessary or desirable to do so.

A's objective is known only to him. Neither B nor the rest of the group are aware of it.

Repetition continues throughout in the same way as before. Once again, the actors are reminded that they must emotionally own and embody both the objective and the activity, so that we begin to get a sense of an embryonic character rather than an actor doing an exercise.

The Objective and Activity Exercise is classic Meisner. Its purpose is to start introducing a stronger fictional element to the given circumstances, so that the actors can begin the transition towards text, character and story. At this point, of course, we are still in the grey area between real and imaginary worlds.

As you start this exercise, you will probably experience a certain confusion about the difference between self and character. 'Am I a character or am I myself?' you may want to know. The clearly fictional nature of the tasks suggests a character, yet you have none of the information and backstory that might confer upon you the permissions of 'being someone else'.

Paraphrasing Meisner, I remind you all that there is no clear dividing line between you and a character. The moment you walk into the acting space and start doing things which are suggested to you either by a teacher or by a written text, then on some level you have become another character; but the character is still yourself, although in different circumstances. If you are playing the role of Irina in Chekhov's *Three Sisters* and have undertaken extensive preparation and rehearsal, it is likely that you will have tried to penetrate as deeply as possible into the world of pre-Revolutionary provincial Russia, and this community in particular. You will have put on different clothes, and you may have changed your way of speaking and moving, but in the end, it will still be *your* body, *your* thoughts, *your* emotions and *your* impulses that the audience sees.

To walk into a space and take on a simple activity or a simple objective is really no different. For the purposes of the exercise, the character is still you, but this is a fictional you who loves making patterns with chairs, or who has a burning need to be considered beautiful. As with Irina's life and desires, all we have to do is understand and buy in to those needs. As actors, we have (or should have) the capacity to take on causes, needs, obsessions, cravings and make them our own. We understand what it is to need things and to search for things, so all we have to do is transfer the emotion that governs our own deepest needs onto the fictional objective.

So you look again at the concept of the actor in the space, and you start to create a new definition. The space is a place of possibility. It is also a place of risk, but the risk, like the possibility, lies within the safe boundaries of the space. In your real lives, you spend a lot of time making sure you are safe, looking over your shoulder and avoiding for the most part situations where you might get emotionally hurt. You have become so suspicious that you expect danger from every quarter, and this attitude has become so embedded in your body and habits that when you do find yourselves in a space that offers the possibility of a more open and daring modus operandi, you cannot find it in yourself. 'Give me a character,' you shout, 'and I'll do it.'

This is hardly new, of course. You are all familiar with the idea of people playing multiple roles in real life too, in order to release or give voice to aspects of themselves they somehow can't access as 'themselves'. Very often these role-plays use costume, a different voice, and of course a different audience from that which the role-player would probably regard as their 'real life'. Many actors also build a character at least partly through 'externals'. It is not that I have any problem with this, I just feel you need to find a greater flexibility, so that you no longer need to move so far from yourself in order to discover yourself. The space should be safe enough that, merely by walking into it and committing to a single simple idea, you can access new and exciting aspects of self.

To succeed in this exercise, you need to respond to its demands. If you are B, ask yourself whether you recognise within yourself a designer, an artist, someone whose psyche expressed in physical objects could be of value. If you are A, think about whether you have any concept of yourself as a beautiful person, either inwardly or outwardly, or at least whether you would like it to be so. These are essential questions actors have to ask when confronted with any character or story, in order to find a connection between the character and the self.

You may also need to take some time to exercise your imagination by practising a simple form of what Meisner called 'daydreaming'. This is merely a few moments of private reflection, during which you allow mental pictures and the associated emotions to form around the fictional objective and activity. This is a very natural human process. In your own lives you probably spend time imagining doing something or experiencing something that hasn't happened yet (or indeed may never happen), and you may experience quite real emotions in response to your daydream. As actors, you can use the daydream in the same way – to open up an emotional response to a fictional idea.

Example 3

Actors A and B start to work with the objective and activity described above. B is genuinely creative with the chairs. She experiments with shapes and symmetry, order and chaos. When A enters, B immediately sees him as a disruptive element within her creative space, and quickly becomes genuinely angry, especially when A attempts to help her, to join her in the creative process. Despite B's anger, A remains vulnerable, needy, and as she rejects him, the need grows.

Eventually, B softens towards A, responding in a human way to his need. A is encouraged, and grows bold, eventually daring once again to help B with the chairs. To start with, B tolerates it, but soon gets exasperated. A becomes rather charmingly submissive, and eventually B invites him to take a limited role in the chair-setting, which he does eagerly. Little by little, A's role grows, and (continuing to pursue his objective) he experiments with the use of his own body as part of the design. All the while both actors are constantly observing and repeating, although all their observations are now charged with their attitude towards one another and with their underlying objectives.

By the time they stop, A has not achieved his objective, but that does not matter. What matters is that he has worked with it and allowed it to energise his actions. What matters still more is that both actors have allowed themselves to give in physically and viscerally to the relationship. This is something that many actors find hard to do, especially out of character. For B it is a matter of being torn between the task she is doing and a certain fascination (and sometimes exasperation) with A. For the group watching it is clear that her choices are entirely defined by real moments in the relationship, and the improvisation becomes compelling to watch.

In a nutshell, if the exercise is successful, what two actors achieve is the combination of an embodied need or desire, with a genuine openness to one another. Within this simple formula lies the secret of good acting. As audience members, you need to believe not only that the actor is mentally, physically, spatially and emotionally living within the character's story, but also that the story is unfolding and playing out in real time before our eyes.

The relative simplicity of this exercise, compared with, say, a scene from a Chekhov play, should allow you to commit to a simple fiction without having to embody vast amounts of information relating to the history of the character and the world of the play. You should be careful not to underestimate the significance of these simple tasks and objectives. In themselves they are not world-shattering, yet if you can find that part of yourself that responds to them emotionally or creatively, while at the same time applying your skills from the early repetition exercises, then you will quickly acquire tools and habits which should serve you well when you start to work on text.

Example 4

The next couple have different tasks. B's activity is to write a letter – not a pretend letter, but a real letter to real person (in other words, a personal letter he would genuinely like to write). A's objective is for B to notice and comment on his new top. To aid him in this, he actually puts a colourful top on over his blacks.

A immediately commits to the idea of needing attention and affirmation, and becomes physically available to the task, which soon leads to an accompanying vulnerability. He flaunts himself before B, smiles, makes B look at him, lies down in front of him, and demands attention. B, on the other hand, does all he can to shut him out so he can write his letter. Most of his comments are scolding – 'You're in my space,' or 'You're blocking my light.' This is fine as far as it goes, and it establishes the relationship well.

Eventually, however, it starts to repeat itself and go round in circles. I stop, and ask B how likely he thinks it is that he will ever be able to write his letter, given the way A is behaving. 'Not very likely,' is the reply. I then ask him what his options are, given that the writing of the letter continues to be an underlying desire. We decide that in order to have any possibility of writing his letter, B will have to find out what it is that A wants, and try to satisfy him, before he can proceed. B could, of course, take A and sling him out of the space, but that option is not permitted.

B then starts to engage with A, and before he knows it, he is captured by his energy and sense of need. A is excited, and cavorts in front of him; B comments on everything he sees, but is unable to identify what A wants. The relationship starts to become a guessing game, at which point I quickly remind B that within repetition we comment on what we see rather than making wild guesses about what our partner is thinking or wanting. Of course, B would like to ask A straight out what he wants, but as with so many situations in life, such a direct approach is simply not possible. What is possible is for B to become immersed in A's mystique and unfathomability, while still nurturing a background desire to write his letter.

At one point, B becomes angry with A's elusiveness and returns to his letter, at which point the repetition continues as follows:

A   (*Disappointed.*) You sat down.

B   (*Huffy.*) I sat down.

A   (*Reproachful.*) You're writing your letter.

B   (*Dismissive.*) I'm writing my letter.

A   (*Sad.*) You're not looking at me.

B   (*Curt.*) I'm not looking at you.

A   (*Almost tearful.*) You're not looking at me.

B   (*Looks at her.*) You're upset.

A	I'm upset.
B	You're not really upset.
A	(*He has his attention now.*) I'm not really upset.
B	You're happy now I'm looking at you.
A	I'm happy now you're looking at me!
B	You're showing off.
A	I'm showing off!
B	You want me to look at you.
A	I want you to look at me!
B	You're expecting something.
A	I'm expecting something.
B	You want me to notice something.
A	I want you to notice something!!
B	You're desperate for me to notice something.
A	I'm desperate for you to notice something!!

Eventually, B does find out what A wants, but again, that is not terribly important in itself. Once again, both actors have entirely forgotten everything outside the world of their improvisation, but just as significantly, they have also allowed their habitual reserve to slip. Lacking as they do a named and scripted character to offer them emotional permissions, they have had no choice but to become emotionally available *as themselves*, albeit within a fictional context.

Example 5

Raising the stakes a little, I give the next A the objective to make B cry (again, B is not told of this objective), while B has the task of drawing an accurate and detailed plan of the space.

As it happens, in real life these two actors have the sorts of personalities which, while not uncommon, often get in the way of their work. Actor A exemplifies the type of person who in real life wants to be liked, and who shies away from any role that requires him to access or reveal a measure of cruelty or brutality. By contrast, Actor B is quite reserved and private in real life, and to compensate he has developed a range of accomplished techniques for faking emotion in the acting space.

Both actors seem acutely aware of their peer group and tutor watching, and they mistakenly assume that they are undergoing some sort of test of their abilities rather than an experiential learning process from which everyone present, including myself, will benefit.

Rather than returning to first principles, engaging with the repetition and finding opportunities within the relationship to pursue the objective, A starts to make obvious if ultimately futile choices, such as snatching B's paper, breaking his pencil and even finding and unpacking his bag. A gets B's attention, but far from making him cry, he only manages to induce annoyance and contempt. B (who is anyway very self-critical in his work) assumes these *genuine* feelings are wrong, and starts *pretending* to be upset. Quickly the whole improvisation descends into meaningless dishonesty and we stop. B is sent out of the room in order for us to question A.

When questioned, A is very clear that he finds it impossible to accept the idea of wanting B to cry. Probing further, we discover that he doesn't want anyone to think he's a nasty person. 'So how would you play Richard III?' I ask. 'But he's not me,' comes the reply. The same old issue, but this time I choose not to confront it head-on.

Instead I ask A whether he believes he could ever make B cry – whether such a thing is within his scope. 'In real life?' he asks. 'Wherever,' I reply. He thinks for a moment, then says he thinks he could, but he wouldn't want to. I agree that to set out to do such a thing might be morally indefensible in his personal life, but point out that such rules can't be observed in the acting space.

I emphasise to A that, in any case, an objective of this kind can't be achieved by breaking someone's pencil. Objectives can only be pursued, let alone achieved, by committing to the desire, heart and soul. Most of the time we access this level of commitment by testing and evaluating the obstacle, and then working to overcome it. That is the challenge that often dynamises us and engages our energies.

In this particular case, it has been obvious to everyone watching that B, intent on drawing his plan, has no particular feelings towards A, either positive or negative, other than exasperation and annoyance at his antics. If we are to make someone cry then we first have to make them care. That, then, is the challenge for A.

B comes back in, and, before we start again, I remind him that, although he has a practical task to complete, and although we absolutely do not want him to pretend emotions he does not feel, we also do not want him to put up barriers against A for the sake of it.

This time, A works entirely differently. He does disrupt B's task, but he uses his quite gentle manner to do it as though it is the best thing for B. He sticks to the rules of repetition in that he makes nothing up and comments only on what he sees, but all the time he is working to subvert B's aloofness and disdain.

A   (*Gently taking his pencil.*) You still want to draw.

B   (*Trying to take it back.*) I still want to draw.

A   (*Holding it out of reach.*) You still want to draw.

B   (*Irritated, still trying.*) I still want to draw.

A   (*Putting a hand on B's shoulder.*) You tried to get the pencil.

B   (*Making a grab.*) I tried to get the pencil.

A   (*Still holding it out of reach.*) It doesn't really matter to you.

B   (*Stopping.*) It doesn't really matter to me.

A   You don't really care.

B   I don't really care.

A   You stopped trying to get it.

B   I stopped trying to get it.

A   You stopped trying to get it.

B   You want me to try again.

A   I want you to try again.

B   You want me to play.

A   I want you to play.

B   You're smiling at me.

A   I'm smiling at you... You don't want to play.

B   I don't want to play.

A   You don't want to play with me.

B   I don't want to play with you.

A   You're not in the mood.

B   I'm not in the mood.

And so it goes on. A doesn't quite succeed in making B cry, but again, that doesn't matter. By making largely accurate observations about B's shifting feelings moment to moment, A manages to take B out of 'performance mode' and into something much more honest and human. Gradually they establish a level of intimacy and understanding, although every time B starts to become vulnerable he checks himself and pulls back. Towards the end something quite interesting happens:

B   (*Holding out his hand.*) You've still got my pencil.

A   (*Holding the pencil out of reach again.*) I've still got your pencil.

B   You won't give it back.

A   I won't give it back... You *still* want it back.

B   I still want it back.

A   (*Genuinely hurt.*) You still want to draw.

B   (*Gently.*) I still want to draw.

A   (*Hands over the pencil.*) You still want to draw.

B   You're hurt.

A   (*Emotional.*) I'm hurt.

B   (*Moved.*) You don't want me to go.

A   I don't want you to go.

B   You don't want me to go.

A   You put the pencil down.

B   I put the pencil down.

Afterwards, A comments that during the second attempt he made a discovery – he actually understood in himself *why* he wanted to make B cry, which was because he felt B was emotionally closed off from him. A felt vulnerable himself, and therefore wanted B to be equally vulnerable to him.

For actors, this is an important discovery about how objectives, even when apparently imposed from outside, can resonate on a personal level between specific actors. We know that Tuzenbakh in Chekhov's *Three Sisters* loves Irina and wants to marry her, but the actor playing that part has to understand what that means to him, and how her attitude affects him, otherwise he will end up playing a generic idea of love rather than being part of a specific relationship.

In real life, you have all sorts of objectives, some of which you may attack head-on, while others may be pursued less directly, largely because in your own life you understand the complexity of relationships and the need to approach certain situations carefully. A simple objective such as running for a bus can be pursued in a direct and physical way, whereas a psychological objective such as getting someone to go on a date with you may take careful handling. One thing is certain, however – objectives are almost always best achieved by first establishing a close and responsive connection with the other person. Repetition and close observation of someone else are an excellent way of shifting your conscious focus from your own need to someone else's, and it is only by observing and responding to changes in that other person, moment by moment, that you can get what you want.

Example 6

The next A wants the B to dance with him. B has the task of unlacing his shoes and re-lacing them in a different style (we line up several other pairs of shoes in case this task runs out).

These two very quickly slip into role-playing. B becomes the 'straight man' (in this case, slightly stern and bad-tempered) and A becomes the 'clown'. There is a lot of facial acting, demonstrating and mime to try and get the message across, but each actor gets steadily more locked into his role, until it is clear that they have reached a stalemate, and no further progress can be made.

I advise them both not to try and create a whole character or archetype out of one task or one objective, but to let the characters grow out of the relationship. Interestingly, when they start again we still see traces of these roles (which are in fact close to the actors' own personalities), but we can now also see how they both emerge from and are challenged by the relationship. At times, B's seriousness does create a more playful counter-reaction in A, but at other times A is forced to get onto B's level in order to be taken seriously by him. Similarly, as the relationship progresses, B is infected by A's energy and enthusiasm, and A does ultimately get B to dance.

The point here, I feel, is that although you may (quite naturally) interpret a task or objective through an aspect of your own personality, you should not crystallise this into a fixed archetype, but instead see it as a useful starting point from which the relationship can genuinely be explored (in this case, through repetition). Again, we are not attempting to write stories but continuing to build the habit of connecting to the other actor and making that connection the main source of our creativity.

Example 7

Raising the stakes a little, I ask the next B to draw a portrait of someone in the room, while the A's objective is for B to hold him. Once again, it is as though these two actors have identified the 'story' of the scene they are going to play, and they start to deliver it to us like a pair of performers rather than working directly from desire, vulnerability and the responses of the other actor. I remind them that they are actors, not playwrights, and that this task is not about playing out predetermined narratives.

Once they have got beyond this, they fall into another error, which is to play out an idea of the relationship, with B as the strong, protective figure and A as the weak, needy one. This would be fine as a starting point, but it is clear that these parameters have been drawn up at the start, and there is no room for shift. A uses emotive comments such as 'You don't care,' which are not genuine observations, and prompt B to switch off.

After more discussion, A stops playing a character and starts to be genuinely vulnerable, working off B's apparent indifference and concentration on her task, and keeping his comments in the realm of moment-to-moment observation.

A   You're not looking at me.

B   (*Busy drawing.*) I'm not looking at you.

A   You're trying to get your picture right.

B   I'm trying to get my picture right.

A   You've got your back to me. (*Moves into her eyeline.*)

B   You're in my way.

A   I'm in your way.

B   You're in my way!

A   You want me to get out of the way.

B   I want you to get out of the way.

A   You thought about moving yourself then.

B   I thought about moving myself then.

A   You chose not to.

B   I chose not to... You want something.

A   I want something.

B   You want me to guess what it is.

A   I want you to guess what it is.

B   You want me to guess what it is.

A   You know what it is.

B   I know what it is.

A   You know what it is.

B   I know what it is.

A   You don't want to give it.

B   I don't want to give it. (*She starts drawing again.*)

A   You don't want to give it. (*He is very upset.*)

B   (*Horrified.*) You're crying.

This is a much more truthful dialogue, partly because the emotions and responses are unforced, and partly because it is rooted in facts and genuine observations. When confronted with A's neediness, B feels uncomfortable and unable to offer anything, and although A's emotion doesn't change that, it makes B feel alienated and trapped, and she becomes panicked and vulnerable within that state. There is no conscious storytelling on the part of the actors, but this resembles a scene played out at the end of a long relationship, in which one party is moving on and the other wants everything to stay the same.

We let the improvisation run on, and eventually A calms down, partly because he perceives that B is distressed and no longer indifferent. However, B doesn't offer A what he wants, and quickly returns to her drawing. A is now angry, but his anger shuts her down completely and the relationship comes to an end.

Although Actor B's final shutdown might have been understandable within the arc of that particular scene, you still have to remind yourselves that Meisner exercises are first and foremost training exercises seeking to free your impulses and keep you open, responsive and vulnerable to other actors. The habit of shutting down and retiring to safe places has to be constantly challenged, not because people in real life don't shut down, but because within these exercises you need constantly to be taking the road less travelled, challenging yourselves, breathing, and choosing the difficult option. There is not just one open/closed switch within us – there are many.

Example 8

In the final improvisation in this exercise, I give A a 'want' that can scarcely be called an objective, since he doesn't really have any way of achieving it, which is that he wants B to die. B has the mundane task of counting all the floorboards in the room.

With no practical course of action to pursue (obviously, he can't actually kill him), A is forced to let the repetition take its course. From the start it is clear that A is deeply disturbed by his task, so much so that he spends a lot of time choking back emotion. B perceives this and is puzzled by it, but can't fathom it. Comments from B such as 'You're waiting for something,' affect A very strongly, although again he stifles the emotion. The result is a scene loaded with tension, in which B ultimately tries to help and support A. In the light of his 'want', this is too much for A, and he breaks down. It is a dark and uneasy scene, but its power lies in the fact that the actors are genuinely transfixed by one another.

By the time you have experienced this exercise, and observed others doing it, you will probably have understood something new, which is how the actor can genuinely focus his needs and desires within another actor, making that actor the constant barometer of his success or failure. The actor wants something and reads signals from the other actor, and in the moment of comment we understand the gap between what is desired and what has been received. Thereby is the fictional objective linked to real observable moments, and itself made real.

7

The Knock
on the Door

'Preparation is that device which
permits you to start your scene
or play in a condition of
emotional aliveness'

The Knock on the Door

The Knock on the Door exercise provides the final bridge between repetition exercises and text. Although repetition forms the backbone for this exercise too, you are also supplied with detailed information about your character's given circumstances and past relationship to the other character. This means that every choice you make within the improvisation must be both truthful in the moment and believable for that character within those fictional circumstances, just as you would want it to be when playing a scripted scene.

However successful you may have been with the earlier repetition exercises, there is a danger that, once you begin to work with characters, detailed backstories and concrete situations, all your learning to date is in danger of being abandoned in favour of old presentational habits, as you strive to deliver the story of the scene rather than responding to the reality of each moment. The following preparatory exercise will help you to retain your newly acquired habit of prioritising the moment over the story:

The Simple Backstory Exercise

Once again working simultaneously in pairs, two actors each imagine that their partner is an ex-lover or close friend, with whom they had a painful break-up five years previously and whom they haven't seen since until this unexpected encounter. They give themselves fictional names to maintain a separation between their own lives and this fictional world.

This is the first of the exercises that uses any kind of backstory or character history, so it is advisable to spend a little time in the 'daydream' – allowing the imagination to range freely over moments in the relationship, including the feelings that may have been present when it finally ended. Most actors will have experiences of their own they can draw on directly, but these should merge freely with more creative, imagined scenarios.

Most actors are able to attack this exercise with the energy and sense of expectation that is clearly rooted in the backstory. However, because you are now so used to repeating and observing, you mustn't make the mistake of letting the given circumstances become the action. Instead, the given circumstances must just be allowed to be there, and somehow the story will emerge in an unforced way through the *detail* of the repetition and the connection you forge with each other.

By now you should have become largely self-instructing on the basic Meisner rules. Provided that you keep faith with your new technique and avoid 'story writing', you should find yourself working from inside the relationship, and doing what anyone would do in that situation – which is to minutely observe the other person in order to pick up the vital signals that tell you just how open and intimate you can afford to be with this person.

This exercise is an important 'litmus test' to show you how far you have absorbed and taken ownership of the new habits. Through it you can get a fairly accurate idea of where you stand on Meisner Technique – in other words, whether you have separated and compartmentalised the repetition exercises, or actually allowed them to change your whole attitude towards the acting space. It is important to be honest about this and to listen to those observing you. If you want to proceed further with Meisner Technique, then you need to accept that your whole way of operating with other actors in conventional rehearsal situations may have to change. This is possibly the biggest challenge that you will encounter within Meisner training, and it should be faced as openly and honestly as possible.

The Knock on the Door

This is one of Meisner's own original exercises. It is a big step forward, marking our first venture into the world of simple concrete fictions, although repetition is still used as the basis for the dialogue.

This exercise is based on the same principles as the Objective and Activity exercise you have done previously, in that one actor with a strong objective interrupts another who is in the middle of a task, literally by knocking at their door. The difference is that here there is much more detail within the given circumstances. Both actors have character names, backstories and a measure of information about their previous relationship and personalities.

The other new rule is that, although the dialogue improvised within this exercise continues to observe the repetition structure as before, a certain divergence from repetition is now permitted – although the actors must always return to the repetition. This will sometimes take the form of a statement a character makes about himself or his needs, so that you don't end up with cryptic guessing games, or a question that needs to be asked. Occasionally we will see an impulsive burst of anger or some other emotion that is verbalised. But any divergence that arises as an impulse from the interaction (rather than from an actor's desire to move the story on or control its direction) is permitted, in order to make the dialogue more natural and maintain the connection between the conditioning forces and the immediacy of the moment.

The scenario below, and those following, are just examples. They can be used by Meisner teachers in this form, or they can form the stimulus for creating new scenarios. It is important that all such scenarios offer sufficient complexity within the given circumstances to ensure that the outcome of the improvisations is not a foregone conclusion. On the other hand, too much background detail may be hard to absorb all at once, so the salient facts of the backstories must be simple, clear and comprehensible.

Scenario 1

The characters are called AMANDA *and* CHRIS. *It is evening in* AMANDA's *London flat.* AMANDA *is in the process of setting up a small theatre company with Arts Council funding, and in this moment is trying to get to grips with the Disability Discrimination Act. She has an important funding interview the following day upon which the whole project depends, and which will include questions on DDA compliance.*

CHRIS *lives in a flat upstairs. He is a fairly attractive man with whom she has previously had the odd date. However, he is a bit of a waster: he is a part-time session musician but with no real job. He never has any money, and he has previously borrowed all sorts of things from her. He often comes down just to cadge a beer.*

This time, although he is happy to have the beer, he has a much stronger objective, which is to get her to go out clubbing. He has stayed in all week for lack of money, and is desperate to have a night out.

Despite her reservations about him, and the fact that she often has to foot the bill, AMANDA *is usually happy to go out with him, as he is a very entertaining person to be with.*

Within this exercise, the given circumstances are not suggestions but absolutes, so you will need to think carefully about the circumstances that have led up to this moment. If you are playing Amanda, you will have to spend some time fleshing out her circumstances and making them your own creation. For example, you may decide that she has previously been employed as assistant director in a large theatre company on quite a good salary, and that she is taking a considerable risk setting up her own company. You may think about the work she has put in so far and the consequences of the interview the next day failing. To stimulate what we will call your 'emotional imagination', you could draw on parallel situations in your own life where you have worried about failing to achieve something important.

If you are playing Chris, you might seem to have the easier task, but then again, as an actor in training you are used to getting up very early, working hard all day and evening, and barely having time or energy for socialising. It may be hard for you to imagine an aimless, slow-paced lifestyle, but perhaps you could think back to a former period in your life when you had a lot of time at home on your own and often felt bored and lonely. If this doesn't work, you might think of someone else you know whose lifestyle resembles Chris's, so you can capture something of the rhythm and visuals of his world.

The time spent thinking though the *implications* of the given circumstances is always crucial to the actor. If you haven't thought through, understood, and on some level emotionally reacted to the situation and stakes, then your work will be superficial and your understanding will lack embodiment. Up to this point, the exercises have only used given circumstances that are contained within the present space and immediate relationship. Now, as with written texts, you have to deal with the *conditioning forces*, which derive from the circumstances and context of the scene. Allowing yourself to find a connection with these before you start is what Meisner called 'emotional preparation', although it is something with which any student of Stanislavsky will also be familiar. It is a simple process, but an essential one.

Your group can also be useful in fleshing out the detail of the given circumstances. They may have personal experiences and insights that can stimulate your imagination. Hearing their stories, and the feelings and events associated with them, can often help you find a personal connection with the character.

In the last chapter, I touched on the notion of the 'daydream'. This is an important concept for the actor as you struggle to take on fictional situations as your own. Meisner remarked that 'preparation is a kind of daydreaming', by which he meant that a logical understanding of the given circumstances, intention and emotional stakes of the characters, can get you only so far. You also have to let the imagination connect on a personal level. A group dialogue can help with this, but before playing a scene you also need to spend time privately thinking through the character's feelings and state of mind, often by imagining circumstances in your own life that might stimulate a similar emotion. In this way you can understand, in the moment before starting the scene, what it physically feels like for the character to be in that situation.

This personalisation is called the 'as if', and you can use it within the 'daydreaming' stage of your preparation to stimulate a connection. What should be made clear, however, is that this is not quite the same as the Stanislavskian technique of 'emotion memory'. The 'as if' does not have to be about things that have actually happened in your life – it could be about things that *might* happen. In other words, you are using real things in your life, with which you already have an emotional connection, to help you understand on a real and visceral level how a character might feel.

The personal fiction you use to make that connection does not, of course, have to be directly related to the scenario of the play, because that set of circumstances may not contain the right stimuli for you. But you cannot go into the space and play from within imaginary circumstances that are *not* those of the play or scenario, so the 'as if' has to be seen not as a substitute for the actual scenario, but as a springboard into it – a way of making you respond to the character's predicament. Meisner described this as finding 'emotional clarity'.

Example 1 (based on Scenario 1)

The actor playing Chris has a naturally cheeky personality, and is used to overstepping boundaries, using charm to get his way. From the start, his actual personality, as one might expect, becomes the basis for his character's attitude and strategies. The improvisation begins as follows:

> AMANDA *sits on the sofa, feet up, reading the Disability Discrimination Act booklet. There is a Knock on the Door. She is exasperated, but goes to answer it, booklet in hand.*
>
> CHRIS   You're busy.
>
> AMANDA   I'm busy... You came in!
>
> CHRIS   I came in.
>
> AMANDA   You came in.
>
> CHRIS   You're in a mood.
>
> AMANDA   I'm in a mood??!
>
> CHRIS   You're in a mood.
>
> AMANDA   You sat down.
>
> CHRIS   I sat down.

AMANDA   You're staying.

CHRIS   I'm staying... You look fantastic.

AMANDA   I look fantastic.

CHRIS   You look fantastic.

AMANDA   I look fantastic.

CHRIS   You picked up that book.

AMANDA   I picked up that book.

CHRIS   You're trying to read it.

AMANDA   I'm trying to read it!

CHRIS   You want me to go?

AMANDA   I want you to go.

CHRIS   You want me to go.

AMANDA   You're not going.

CHRIS   I'm not going.

AMANDA   Do you want a beer?

CHRIS   Do I want a beer!

AMANDA   One beer and then you go.

CHRIS   One beer and then I go.

AMANDA   Beer's in the fridge. (*Sits down.*)

CHRIS   Beer's in the fridge... You sat down.

AMANDA   I sat down...

CHRIS   You sat down.

AMANDA   I sat down.

CHRIS   You picked up your book.

AMANDA   I picked up my book... You're getting the beer.

CHRIS   I'm getting the beer.

AMANDA   You mustn't talk.

CHRIS   I mustn't talk... You're not having one?

AMANDA   I'm not having one.

The Knock on the Door exercise allows you to use statements, imperatives and questions that go beyond direct observation of one another, but from this example you can see that the actors' training keeps bringing them back to the simple physical happenings and observed reactions, so that for the most part the dialogue still resembles Standard and Psychological Repetition. It is from those observations that you can find unexpected detail within the relationship, which makes it more real for the group watching. In the example above, when Chris comments that Amanda has sat down after offering him a beer, it is clear that he wants her to treat him as a guest and get him the beer. Her action of sitting down, and his reaction to it, are real events, yet they emerge from the actors' internalisation of their given circumstances, which allow them both to act and react in character and within the situation.

You might be dealing with a fuller set of circumstances and more definite characters, but by continuing to observe in a detailed way you can make these improvisations genuine exploratory processes rather than presentations. You need at all costs to avoid shortcuts and manipulation, as in the example below.

Example 1 continued

Having got his beer, CHRIS *sits on the end of the sofa and watches her reading.*

CHRIS   You're busy.

AMANDA   I'm busy... You spoke to me.

CHRIS   I spoke to you.

AMANDA   You spoke to me.

CHRIS   You don't want me to speak to you.

AMANDA   I don't want you to speak to me.

CHRIS   You don't want me here.

AMANDA   I don't want you here.

CHRIS   You don't want to go clubbing with me.

AMANDA   I don't want to go clubbing with you.

CHRIS   You want to read that book.

AMANDA   I want to read this book!

CHRIS   You don't want to read that book.

He takes the book from her.

AMANDA   You took my book away!!!

CHRIS   I took your book away.

The problem here lies in Amanda's actual response to having her book snatched away. Despite her emotional preparation, she had difficulty feeling what she thought she should be feeling in response to this event. Her actual feeling in that moment, as she admitted afterwards, was one of slight amusement at the sheer cheek of the gesture. However, aware as she was of the given circumstances, she censored that feeling, and pretended to be outraged and annoyed. This continued, but since the feeling was not real, all we experienced was a slightly whining tone, a slack body, and a series of 'bids' – faked head, hand and facial gestures aimed at reinforcing a fake emotion. The dialogue continued as follows:

AMANDA   (*Whining.*) You took my book away!

CHRIS   (*Observing her closely.*) You don't really care.

AMANDA   (*Pretending outrage.*) I don't really care??!!

CHRIS   (*Convinced he is right.*) You don't really care.

AMANDA   (*Still pretending.*) I don't really care??!!

The actor playing Chris is a good observer, relatively unafraid of stating the truth as he sees it, and he quickly dismantles

Amanda's fake reaction. From his point of view, this is a truthful response, but her continued pretence has the immediate effect of lowering the stakes and making the scene much less tense and much more predictable. We can see already that Amanda will quickly cave in and go clubbing. Afterwards, the actor playing Amanda is perplexed and a little defensive about the group's comments. 'How do I work within the given circumstances if I have to be honest but I don't feel it?' she asks.

The answer is that Meisner improvisations are not performances. Although it is certainly the job of the actor to bring an embodied sense of the given circumstances to the playing of a dialogue, whether scripted or improvised, within Meisner Technique this should not happen by forcing or faking emotions to fit the circumstances, but through a gradual process of developing the relationship and understanding the world of the play through constant replaying and adjustment.

It is perfectly feasible that the character of Amanda, despite the pressure on her, could be momentarily amused by Chris's action in snatching the book. However, there is a great deal of difference between the *actor* thinking outside of the scene, deciding that this emotion is invalid and faking something different; and the *character* suddenly realising where this is going and pulling herself back. In the first instance, the body reacts to the dishonesty and shuts down; in the second, the body energises as the imaginary conditioning forces kick in, and the initial emotion is overlaid with a stronger counter-emotion. This can only happen if the actor has been brave enough to trust both her genuine feelings and the given circumstances that she has previously internalised.

The upshot of this is that you cannot direct yourself and act at the same time. If, within an improvisation, the given circumstances are not real enough in your imagination to affect your impulses and responses, you can't fix this while improvising the scene – you simply have to learn from it and try to fix it later.

Example 1 continued

The actors begin the scene again, and this time it becomes much more complex, because although Chris's needs and tactics are relatively straightforward, Amanda is pulled in different directions. Part of her responds to Chris and is anyway bored by the DDA booklet, but another part of her is determined to be allowed to continue with her task.

In the event, something interesting happens, which is that Chris makes a serious mistake by not giving her the book back when she asks for it, thereby denying her the opportunity to make the choice for herself. Instead he holds it out of her reach and taunts her with her dilemma. Suddenly, quite unexpectedly, the actor playing Amanda experiences a rush of fury and emotion at being treated this way, and explodes at him:

AMANDA   (*Furious and tearful.*) Give me my fucking book!

CHRIS   (*Startled.*) Give you your book?

AMANDA   Yes, give me the fucking book, you arsehole!

CHRIS   Arsehole?

     He gives her the book.

AMANDA   (*Still in tears.*) You gave me the book.

CHRIS   I gave you the book... You're crying.

AMANDA   I'm crying.

CHRIS   It matters to you.

AMANDA   It really matters to me.

CHRIS   It really matters to you.

AMANDA   You're disappointed.

CHRIS   I'm disappointed.

AMANDA   We can go out on Friday.

CHRIS   We can go out on Friday.

AMANDA	We can go out on Friday.
CHRIS	You want to make me feel better.
AMANDA	I want to make you feel better.
CHRIS	You want me to go now.
AMANDA	(*Slightly tearful again.*) I want you to go now... You looked at the door.
CHRIS	I looked at the door.
AMANDA	You're going towards the door.
CHRIS	I'm going towards the door... You feel guilty.
AMANDA	I feel guilty.
CHRIS	You mustn't feel guilty.
AMANDA	I mustn't feel guilty... You're opening the door.
CHRIS	I'm opening the door.

And so it ends. The actor playing Amanda is elated, feeling she has had a personal breakthrough – and in one way she has, but not in the way she thinks. She has not suddenly become a more open or emotional person – that would be very unlikely to happen in one exercise – but she has started to learn how to explore a scene through interaction with other actors, rather than trying to serve it up fully prepared.

The truthfulness of your interactions can also serve to support your belief in the given circumstances, so that by a gradual process of 'layering,' the fictional world becomes more and more accessible within the scene.

This example highlights one of the biggest problems actors encounter when they try to act truthfully. Even in the early repetition exercises, where there is no play or storyline to be delivered, you may find it hard to be truthful about what you see, and to respond to it organically. Once you start to work with characters and backstories, there is an increased danger that you will sacrifice the truth of the moment to what is somehow considered to be the greater truth of the story. In other words, you consider it better to fake a reaction, or pretend to see something you don't actually see, than to disrupt the direction in which the story or play needs to go. Many actors get round this problem by not really responding to their fellow actors at all, finding instead internal technical routes to whatever preordained emotional place the script requires.

In the end, this can only lead to 'set-piece' acting, which is the very thing Meisner Technique seeks to avoid. It also leads to a self-perpetuating mutual mistrust among actors, whereby they automatically assume (whether they admit it or not) that they are better off relying on personal technique than genuine interaction to steer them through a scene.

Such lack of trust can only be reversed if actors practise the art of giving up control and learning to work with the truthful interactive moment. Above all, this involves training yourself to respond to what you *actually see* rather than *responding to the sign that is held up*. By this I mean that you should train yourself to react to your fellow actors in the same way that you react to other human beings in real life. In real life, you do not just listen to words – you respond to body language, tone of voice and countless other signifiers which communicate to you what a person is thinking and feeling. In the acting space, there is a tendency for you to see the vocal and physical gestures of others merely as 'cues' for a predetermined response, which causes you to switch off your sensors and respond to the signpost rather than the human being.

One of the most useful aspects of Meisner training is that the work almost always takes place with two actors in the space and the rest observing. The observation, as I have mentioned, is as important for your training as the participation, since it

allows you to experience emotionally and viscerally the difference between a truthful moment and one which is contrived.
When you watch two actors, however good their vocal and physical technique, going through the motions of a dramatic scene,
you probably feel sceptical and a little bored – although you
might find it hard to acknowledge those feelings. A moment of
unexpected truth, on the other hand, wakes you up, sharpens
your senses and gets the adrenalin flowing.

The Knock on the Door exercise gives you the opportunity,
free from the pressures of the rehearsal room, to explore your
own habits and to train yourself to trust your real response
rather than imposing a fictional one.

Scenario 2

The scene is REBECCA's *London flat, on a Sunday afternoon.*
REBECCA *is looking for a tiny screw which holds her glasses
together and which has fallen out onto the floor. Without her
glasses, she is unable to prepare for an important meeting at
work.* PAUL, *who lives upstairs, has come down to ask if he can
borrow her car that evening to go to the station and collect his
mother who is coming to stay for a few days (she lives in the
wilds of Yorkshire and can't stand Underground trains).*

In the past, PAUL *has been a good friend and a listening ear
following some of* REBECCA's *disastrous relationships.*

*A particular conditioning force affecting the scene is that,
although* REBECCA *has previously lent him the car, she is feeling
angry with him because he refused to lend her some chairs the
week before when she was giving a dinner party, on the grounds
that his chairs were antiques and might get spoiled.*

REBECCA *struggles to maintain order in her life, both at home
and at work. Although in many ways good at her job, she often
has to work through the night to meet deadlines and to arrive on
time to appointments. She does a lot of things at the last minute,
and is often stressed as a result.*

By contrast, PAUL *is very methodical, organised and tidy. He is obsessed with his clothes and the look of his flat, and can't bear any kind of disruption to his space. He likes* REBECCA, *but can't understand her scattiness.*

PAUL *is slightly mean with money, and he is reluctant to pay for a taxi to collect his mother, which is why he is asking* REBECCA *for the car.*

Example 2 (based on Scenario 2)

In the dialogue below, the actors have found a connection with the given circumstances, and the tension between them is palpable. They are able to observe each other and respond very effectively:

PAUL   You finally opened the door.

REBECCA   I finally opened the door.

PAUL   You only opened it a bit.

REBECCA   I only opened it a bit.

PAUL   You don't want me to come in.

REBECCA   I don't want you to come in.

PAUL   You're busy.

REBECCA   I'm busy.

PAUL   Look, I need to borrow your car.

REBECCA   You need to borrow my car?

PAUL   I need to borrow your car.

REBECCA   Sorry, no.
          She starts to shut the door

PAUL   You're shutting the door!

REBECCA   I'm shutting the door.

PAUL   You're pissed off with me.

REBECCA   I'm pissed off with you.

She shuts the door and resumes her task. PAUL
stands uncertainly and then knocks again.
After a pause she answers.

REBECCA   I'm sorry.

PAUL   You're sorry.

REBECCA   I've lost a screw from my glasses.

PAUL   You've lost a screw from your glasses?

REBECCA   I've lost a screw from my glasses.

PAUL   You need help.

REBECCA   I need help... You're coming in.

PAUL   I'm coming in.

REBECCA   You're looking for the screw.

PAUL   I'm looking for the screw.

REBECCA   You're looking in the wrong place.

PAUL   I'm looking in the wrong place.

REBECCA   You're trying to be helpful.

PAUL   I'm trying to be helpful.

REBECCA   You're looking for the screw.

PAUL   I'm looking for the screw.

REBECCA   You're looking because you want the car.

PAUL   I'm looking because I want the car??

REBECCA   You don't want me to think that.

PAUL   I don't want you to think that.

REBECCA   You stopped looking.

PAUL   I stopped looking... You don't want me to
look.

REBECCA   I don't want you to look.

PAUL   You're angry.

REBECCA   I'm angry... You know why I'm angry.

PAUL   I know why you're angry.

REBECCA   You know why I'm angry... You got up.

PAUL   I got up.

At this point, the actor playing Paul stops trusting the interaction, possibly because the improvisation has moved onto an emotional level and he no longer feels safe with it. Rather than following his impulse, he tenses and sits back on the sofa looking despondent. The group is disappointed – they can all see how contrived and self-consciously theatrical this last move is.

REBECCA   You sat on the sofa.

PAUL   I sat on the sofa.

The actor playing Rebecca is confused. This is the first point in the improvisation that she has been faced with a palpably false response, and she doesn't quite how to deal with it. Knowing the other actor as she does, she is probably aware that it is his habit to evade in this way, yet she is unsure whether to see his gesture for what it is – his character trying to manipulate her character, or to separate actor from character and accept the faked emotion as real. To the group's disappointment, she chooses the latter:

REBECCA   You're worried I'll tell you to go.

PAUL   I'm worried you'll tell me to go.

REBECCA   You're trying to think what to do.

PAUL   I'm trying to think what to do.

REBECCA   You put your face in your hands.

PAUL   I put my face in my hands.

At this point, the actor playing Rebecca has had enough. She can stretch her credulity no further, and to the group's relief, she starts to be truthful about what she sees.

REBECCA You're trying to look sorry.

PAUL I'm trying to look sorry.

REBECCA You stopped trying.

PAUL I stopped trying.

REBECCA You're waiting for me to do something.

PAUL I'm waiting for you to do something.

REBECCA You're waiting for *me* to do something.

PAUL I'm sorry about the chairs.

REBECCA You're sorry about the chairs?

PAUL I *am* sorry about the chairs.

REBECCA You're lying to me!

Slight pause.

PAUL I'm lying to you.

REBECCA You're fucking lying to me.

PAUL You're right, I'm 'fucking' lying to you... Okay, I don't want your 'fucking' car.

REBECCA You don't want my car??

To some extent, the actor playing Paul is also relieved to be exposed. There is nothing more painful for an actor than to find himself trapped in a fake dialogue. Now, however, she sees his evasion as part of the character, and accepts it within the world of the scene. This relaxes him a little, and he is able to open up. His next choice is made in a much more organic way in response to her hostile tone and body language:

PAUL Come on, let's find your screw.

REBECCA Let's find my screw?

PAUL You're surprised.

REBECCA I'm surprised... You're on the floor.

PAUL I'm on the floor.

REBECCA   You're looking for the screw.

PAUL   I'm looking for the screw... You don't want me to.

REBECCA   No, I don't want you to.

This exchange is a good example of how the Meisner-trained actor refuses to respond to the sign held up (in this case 'I'm sorry for refusing to lend you the chairs'), but responds instead to the truth of the body and the voice, which in this case were not convincing. Afterwards, the actor playing Paul says that pretending to be sorry in order to get her car made him feel so bad about himself that he had to look for the screw and *not* ask for the car, just to prove to himself he was a decent person. The actor playing Rebecca, on the other hand, says she wanted him to notice and engage with how she was feeling.

What you can learn from this about objectives is that within the realm of complex relationships, emotions and psychology, you are more likely to achieve an objective by focusing on the other person and responding to how they feel, than by any number of compensatory acts. This might sound like something out of a counselling session, but it is also good advice to the actor. As actors, you have to learn not to fall into the trap of doing everything except the one really important thing, which is *to engage with the other actor.*

The actors playing Rebecca and Paul comment afterwards that, when you allow a moment of observational truth, it is like a knife cutting through the artifice of a 'staged' interaction, making the fictional world suddenly much more real and solid, and allowing you to connect emotionally to its circumstances much more fully.

8 Emotion

'Get your inner life from what the given circumstances suggest'

Emotion

At this point in the Meisner training, it is probably a good idea to talk a little about emotion as an issue in acting. Emotion is probably the single most talked about subject where acting is concerned, arousing more fear and anxiety and generating more myths than any other aspect of the training, particularly among male actors.

If the job of the actor is to embody the character, then clearly the actor has to do what the character does; or, since the character is, to begin with, merely a concept, what the text and director *require* that the character does. Here we have to make the distinction between *doing* and merely *showing*. Where emotion is concerned, this means that the actor is required not just to feel what the character feels, but to find an expression for it that is clear and readable. Whereas in real life many of us experience emotion in quite a muted way – so much so that other people often can't read our emotions – the actor has to be able to communicate his or her genuine emotional states in ways that serve the story and the character.

With Meisner work, of course, you are not expected to generate emotion from within, other than as emotional preparation. What you do have to do is allow other actors to stimulate emotion in you. Many actors have never learned to do this, and employ all manner of substitute indicators to try and convince an audience that they are in a state of high emotion, including a quavery voice, hiding the face, screwing up the facial muscles or shouting very loudly. Such fake acting is usually easy to spot and for the most part leaves the audience cold.

Other actors study imaginative, physical or sensory techniques to gain access to their emotions and achieve emotional release at will. It is probably best to try all of these things within your training, because, as adults, tension and blocks will have built up in all areas of your psycho-physical make-up. There is a great deal of difference, though, between the actor who can generate emotion from within, and the actor who is *emotionally available*, open to allowing another actor to affect him or her emotionally within the context of a scene or improvisation.

With young British actors, especially males, there is also a certain awkwardness about being vulnerable or emotional in public. Within our fairly reserved culture, heightened emotional states are usually reserved for private or domestic contexts, and when they spill out into the public arena they are often met with disapproval and embarrassment. It is possible that some actors have subconscious guilty feelings about genuinely feeling and expressing emotion in their work, as if to do so is in some way offensive and disrespectful to those who are having those experiences in real life.

This rather puritanical attitude is tricky to deal with – especially as many actors are not even aware of it – but it may be useful for a group of actors to spend some time affirming their craft not just as valid creative endeavour, but as part of a social ritual that affirms the world's emotional struggles and makes people feel less alone. The actor's search for emotional truth is therefore a deeply respectful mission, because in seeking to be more real, you are actually less likely to end up misrepresenting, underplaying or belittling serious and difficult subjects.

The Meisner training is one of the techniques that potentially make it easier for you to overcome these habitual reservations. Meisner training does this by making the fictional worlds of the acting space function less like performance and more like real life. The act of becoming and behaving as the character becomes less of a conscious choice and more of an organic process, which happens through the actors' engagement with each other within the boundaries of the narrative.

Emotional Preparation

In the last chapter, I attempted to illustrate the ways in which the Knock on the Door exercise can help you overcome your tendency to manipulate your own responses. Using the same exercise, this chapter will look at how you might prepare for a series of scenarios that make further emotional demands, raising the stakes still further, and require not just significant emotional preparation but considerable emotional courage within the improvisations. You now have to learn how to work with real and powerful emotional impulses, while still remaining within the boundaries of the fictional narrative, its circumstances and imperatives.

Scenario 1

The scene is MARTINE's London flat, midweek, evening. STEVE is an actor living in the north of England. He is staying at the flat of his friend MARTINE for one night, because he has a casting in the West End the following day. He is busy studying the script that the casting director has sent him. MARTINE is out at an evening class. Since his arrival that afternoon he has barely spoken to MARTINE, so knows nothing about her personal life.

ALAN is MARTINE's boyfriend, and they have had a massive row the night before about her suspected infidelity. ALAN comes round to apologise and finds STEVE in the flat. He jumps to the obvious conclusion.

To connect as actors to this scenario and the characters, you would need to start by spending some time discussing the objectives of Steve and Alan. Obviously, each character has a larger and more long-term objective which is present before the knock. In Alan's case, this is to put things right with Martine; in Steve's case it is clearly to do a good reading and get the acting job. In most Knock on the Door scenarios, the characters' most immediate concern is the sub-objective, which kicks in at the point of encounter and which is centred in the other person. In order to achieve his larger objective with Martine, Alan has to get Steve out of the flat. In order to do his work on the script, Steve has to get Alan out of the flat. Each of them is also continually trying to make sense of the other's behaviour. Assuming that neither is the violent type, the scene has to play out psychologically through a series of moment-by-moment observations.

It is very important for an actor to start with the right objective, because, although the objective can change as events unfold, if the actor does not fully believe in or comprehend the objective at the start of the scene, the work will lack the ring of truth both for the actor and ultimately for the observer. If this happens, everything the actor does will be low on energy and clarity. This is because objectives are always centred in the other actor, and they therefore define the attitude that one character has towards another, which in turn dictates the emotional energy, body language, spatial relationship and vocal choices.

Example 1 (based on Scenario 1)

The first time we try this scenario neither of the actors really connects either to the objective or to the given circumstances. Despite our initial preparation, they seem to be relying on the repetition itself to create the tension and energy within the scene, rather than bringing the energy of the given circumstances in with them. Both characters come across as guarded and unforthcoming. Their preparation is incomplete because, although they understand the story and the stakes, they haven't personally and emotionally 'given in' to the circumstances of the scene.

This is a classic example of a lack of emotional preparation, or to be more accurate, the 'right kind' of emotional preparation. There is no point in knowing the given circumstances unless you are also able to *live* imaginatively within them, and the only way you can do that successfully is to use your emotional imagination to access parallel feelings from your own life.

If you are playing the character of Alan, then you will need to start accessing those feelings within you that are about a relationship breaking up. These don't have to be actual memories – most people have at some point had a row with a partner and contemplated breaking up. The visceral feeling of emptiness and fear associated with these thoughts is something that you will probably recognise. Your job as an actor is to unearth those feelings from the place deep within you where they lie buried, and through the daydream, to awaken them.

To do this successfully, you may have to dream up some quite uncomfortable images. If you are playing Alan, you might imagine seeing Martine intimately involved with a new partner, imagine writing her letters and emails and receiving no reply, or any number of other narratives you associate with the end of a relationship. It is very important that the daydream takes you to narratives and the associated feelings, rather than abstract or generalised feelings. The preparation you do must make you need or want something specific, so that you enter the space with an emotion that is active and dynamic.

The other aspect of your preparation must be the manner of your entrance. Clearly Alan expects the door to be opened by Martine, and his whole emotional journey to that point is likely to have been a series of imagined versions of the scene from that point, including at least one in which Martine slams the door in his face because she hasn't forgiven him for the row the night before. By the time you arrive at the door, you will have lived through all of these possibilities in your imagination, which means you will probably be quite agitated and prepared to launch very quickly into your first conciliatory speech – which will make the appearance of Steve come as a much greater shock.

Within almost all of the Knock on the Door scenarios, it is the character who comes in (A) who 'drives' the scene by having the stronger objective. The other character (B) invariably presents the scene-driver (A) with an obstacle, either because of his own objective/activity, or because of some other past circumstance.

Scenarios in which A and B have a shared history require you, if you are playing B, to find your own 'as if', so that you can start the scene with the right feelings towards A. In this scenario, however, Alan and Steve have no past, so the only preparation the actor playing Steve can do relates to the difficulty of finding work as an actor, the tedium of doing other jobs to stay alive, the excitement of getting a casting and the determination to do well.

While these should be easy concepts for the actor playing Steve to relate to, it is unlikely that Steve will be agitated or in a deeply emotional state, since his own ordeal (the casting meeting) is still a few hours off. As with many scenes, here it is the job of the scene-driver to set the emotional tone of the encounter, and the job of the other character to respond.

Emotional preparation, and the daydream in particular, require you to take sufficient time (a few minutes is usually enough) and find a place where you can stand, sit or lie still to allow the imagination to work. If you feel under pressure, your body is likely to tense up, obstruct the breath and stifle the imagination. Only when the body and breath are released can the imagination and the emotions flow.

Example 1 continued

Once both actors have spent some time in the daydream, they are able to start playing with the right emotional energy. This time there is an edge to the scene from the beginning. The actor playing Alan reacts strongly to the presence of Steve, and quickly accesses some quite raw aggression. Once identities have been established, this becomes more overt. Steve reacts to the perceived threat, and the scene temporarily comes to life:

ALAN   You've made yourself at home.

STEVE   I've made myself at home.

ALAN   You're very comfortable.

STEVE   I'm very comfortable??!

ALAN   You're very comfortable.

STEVE   You're very aggressive.

ALAN   I'm very aggressive.

STEVE   You clenched your fists.

ALAN   I clenched my fists... You're scared.

STEVE   I'm scared??

ALAN   You stood up.

STEVE   I stood up.

ALAN   You want to throw me out.

STEVE   I want to throw you out.

ALAN   You nearly stepped forward then.

STEVE   I nearly stepped forward then.

From this point the whole thing gets a bit stuck in a stand-off, from which neither seems able to move on. Unable to leave, unable to fight, they stand and stare at each other. The physicality of the confrontation brings a momentary connection to their bodies, but since this has nowhere to go other than into a physical fight or out of the space, they quickly revert to shuffling and disconnection.

I ask Alan what precisely he is seeing in Steve, and he says he can see a mixture of aggression and confusion. I then ask how this relates to his objective, and he agrees that he is very far away from achieving it. I ask him what he would like to see. After a pause for thought he says 'Guilt, remorse, regret.' I tell him to do the repetition, honestly and without manipulation, but with that objective present in the background. I remind him to breathe and to use his own vulnerability within the given circumstances to allow the scene to take a different direction. We spend a little more time talking about the panic that ensues when we believe we have ruined a relationship unnecessarily and can't find a way to repair it.

After a few false starts, the actor playing Alan begins to make some different choices, but it is clear he finds the process of staying open so terrifying that he is unable to do very much within it. It has an effect on him, however, and the repetition maintains his connection and stops him becoming internally focused. We can see him becoming more and more charged, not in his face and fists this time, but in his body. Suddenly he explodes, leaps from the sofa and hammers on the wall, afterwards collapsing in tears. What follows, however, is very different. The actor playing Alan does not wallow in the emotion, but on the contrary is released by it. Steve has been shocked and moved by Alan's outburst, and the two of them are now able to resolve the central misunderstanding of the scene through an intense and compassionate dialogue which flows as if it had been written.

This stage of the Meisner work can often stimulate emotional explosions, largely because the Knock on the Door exercise is usually such a potent mix of ingredients. Having spent so long learning to stay in the repetition, to trust the three simple tasks of observing, commenting and repeating, and thereby to maintain connection and continuity, you now find yourself applying these skills within a series of increasingly heightened scenarios. In response, you may start to break through emotional barriers, which for some can be an explosive and disconcerting event.

You need to think of this as one part of a long training process. The first time you push beyond the boundaries of long-established 'comfort zones' in your acting work, you may experience a loss of control and find yourself temporarily unable to use the emotions you have released in a useful or creative way. This is hardly surprising – to work with strong emotions without either becoming self-conscious or losing control is a skill that takes both time and courage to keep trying. Repetition, and the habits it engenders, can help you to stay connected and on track even when struggling with powerful and uncomfortable feelings.

A Shared History

The next scenario raises the emotional stakes still further. Here the central conflict is a defining moment within the characters' relationship, which means that both actors have to start with an embodied understanding of the 'stakes' within the scene.

Scenario 2

The scene is NEIL's *London flat, weekday, evening.* NEIL *is preparing a job application for a job in Singapore for which he has been recently headhunted.* NEIL *has a lot of personal debt, and the new job comes with a flat and an excellent salary.*

SHAWN *knocks on the door. He was made redundant from Pernod a year previously with a generous payout. He and* NEIL *have been discussing plans to set up a wine-importing business.* SHAWN *is unaware of* NEIL's *troubled finances, assuming that* NEIL *has a well-paid job, and will be easily capable of putting up his half of the initial outlay.*

NEIL *feels guilty about abandoning* SHAWN, *and has put off telling him about the new job and the fact that he can't afford to join him in the business.*

SHAWN *is excited, because he has an offer of some very cheap warehouse space, but he and* NEIL *will need to get the company set up quickly in order to accept this offer. He has come to urge* NEIL *to speed up the process.*

This is a scenario with a complicated storyline and a lot of information in the backstory. I remind the actors that they may have to diverge quite a lot from pure observation and comment in order to pursue their objectives, and that this is okay, provided repetition remains the backbone of the dialogue. Neil's opening objective might be to find a way of temporarily satisfying Shawn so he can complete his application. Neil's obstacle is that Shawn has come to his flat determined to gain his immediate commitment and agreement.

Example 2 (based on Scenario 2)

The actors' first attempt reminds us of the gulf between understanding the issues intellectually as observers, and actually putting that learning into practice within the space. The actor playing Neil quickly goes into a slightly irrelevant childish and defensive mode, from which nothing can shift him. In other words, he is playing a mood he feels safe with rather than an objective. Meanwhile, the actor playing Shawn starts to make 'bids' on the character, offering us a superficial idea of Shawn rather than working from his inner need. His reactions to Neil's rebuffs seem more like a comic sketch than a serious improvisation.

Unsatisfactory experiences of this kind are very useful in Meisner training, because they show both the actors and the observing group the dangers of trying to play a surface idea rather than an inner truth. One way of finding a closer connection with an imaginary situation is to delve into it, exploring its detail and complexity through 'hot-seating', in which the actor answers a series of questions in character, so that the imagination begins to respond. Here the actor playing Neil is in the hot-seat:

Q   Why have you allowed yourself to be drawn into this business plan?

A   I felt bad that Shawn had lost his job – I wanted to help.

Q   So if you want to help, why not go through with it?

A   I can't. I've got too much debt. I can't take risks like this.

Q   Why don't you tell Shawn the truth?

A   I can't. This business idea is the only thing keeping Shawn going. He would be devastated if I pulled out.

Q	But surely he'd understand if you've got money problems?
A	Shawn's a risk-taker. He'd just think I was being timid. He believes he's going to make a fortune.
Q	But he's got to know some time. When will you tell him?
A	If I get the job in Singapore, I'll make it seem as if I was headhunted, so it won't seem like such a betrayal.
Q	So meanwhile you're prepared to let Shawn carry on putting time and money into this business idea?
A	I don't want him to spend money or make commitments. I just need to stall things.
Q	But Shawn's got an offer of warehouse space he needs to accept. How can that be stalled?
A	I just need to let him know I'm not ready.

By the time you have listened to the questions, thought about them and found an answer, you will probably have begun to experience first-hand the character's fear and moral dilemma, as well as the indefensibility of his actions. Hot-seating is a useful exercise in this case because it forces you to think and speak about the central issue of the scene in the first person, and to negotiate the contradictions.

Example 2 continued

Following an extended hot-seating exercise involving both actors, the second attempt is initially much better. Neil is quite emotionally available, and we can see clearly the cost to him as he ducks and dives around Shawn's direct and driven enthusiasm.

SHAWN	You don't want to talk about it.
NEIL	I don't want to talk about it.
SHAWN	You can't see how important this is!
NEIL	I can't see how important this is.
SHAWN	You can't see how important this is.
NEIL	You're very keen.
SHAWN	I'm very keen.
NEIL	You're excited.
SHAWN	Of course I'm excited!
NEIL	Your voice went squeaky.
SHAWN	My voice went squeaky!
NEIL	You clutched the back of the sofa.
SHAWN	I clutched the back of the sofa... You think I'm overexcited.
NEIL	I think you're overexcited.
SHAWN	You think I'm overexcited.
NEIL	I think you're a bit overexcited.
SHAWN	I've been out of work for a year.
NEIL	You've been out of work for a year.
SHAWN	(*Emotional.*) I've been out of work for a year.

What happens now is that the actor playing Shawn observes himself being emotional, and instead of continuing to pursue the objective, starts to play with the emotion, like a new toy. Almost at once he ceases to be believable, and we start to see the actor rather than the character. Unfortunately, so does the actor playing Neil, and so a promising scene grinds to a halt.

It is notable here that neither actor is emotionally blocked. What we are dealing with in the case of the actor playing Shawn is the deeply embedded habit of presenting and shaping an emotional journey rather than living it, while in the case of the actor playing Neil, there is a tendency to wallow in emotion instead of allowing it to be part of the dynamic of the scene.

The two actors play the scene at least five times more. Each time we stop it is because one or both of them has ceased to trust the reality of the moment and has started to 'watch' himself – and perform. At various points the actors pass though frustration, self-hatred and hatred of the Meisner Technique, but the last time we do the scene something different happens. It is as though our dogged criticism has disillusioned the actors to such an extent that they give up trying to act well, or to act at all.

With the sense of performance removed, the actor playing Neil actually becomes more like himself in real life – vulnerable and compassionate, but also watchful and slightly suspicious. The actor playing Shawn, on the other hand, becomes less polished and more ragged and hesitant. Both actors now have nothing to fall back on but the repetition itself. They know that if they do anything else they will be challenged by the group.

In each case, we start to feel we are getting something much more real. This is a complex scenario, because the characters are not lovers or jealous admirers but potential business partners, which means that the dialogue constantly flits back and forth across the boundary between the formal and the personal, and the emotion is often more subtextual than explicit. The actors' own personalities start to shine through the embryonic characters, not in a contrived way, but quite organically and for the most part appropriately. The actor playing Neil has a tendency to shift into an overtly emotional place, but as the character he realises he has to control that tendency in order to achieve his objective. By contrast, the actor playing Shawn feels safest conversing in a formal and understated way, but has to allow himself to become more raw and impulsive in order to try and motivate Neil. However unformed and exploratory it might be, the work is interesting to watch because there is an inner struggle going on for each actor.

Trusting the Moment

Learning to work with emotion is another aspect of Meisner training. As I mentioned at the beginning of this chapter, there is a great deal of difference between 'wallowing' in a generalised emotional state and being emotionally present. An actor needs to be 'connected' to a fictional situation in the sense of being able to think and feel as the character, and the emotion he feels should be dynamic, constantly changing in response to the other character, and not necessarily overtly expressed. Meisner likened emotion to a river, and rivers are by their nature moving and travelling, rather than standing still.

Scenario 3

This involves two people who are comparative strangers. KYLE, *aged thirty-four, is writing a letter to the council asking to be rehoused because of the violence and drug-dealing in the area.* MICHAEL, *nineteen, knocks on the door. He is terrified because he owes money to a dealer and hasn't got it. He wants to lie low in* KYLE's *flat for a time, just until the dealer's friends go away.*

KYLE *vaguely knows* MICHAEL's *mother, who lives in the block. She is a good woman, but seems to have no control over him. He has seen* MICHAEL *around but never spoken to him.*

Before you attempt a scene of this kind, you need to spend quite a long time talking about its potential pitfalls. It is the kind of scene that might be more conventionally improvised by teenagers in a youth theatre or school drama session. What they would probably be trying to convey, in these contexts, would be the world of urban council estates and drug-dealing, complete with the language, facts and character types. While these are essential background material for a piece of social realism, here you are being asked to do something different – which is to find out whether the human connection between two people can prove stronger than fear or habit.

Example 3 (based on Scenario 3)

Neither of the actors is familiar with this world, so we do spend some time listening to those who have some experience of how it functions. We also have to think about the reality of what might happen to someone who falls foul of drug gangs. We also have to think about Kyle's experience living on the estate. We decide that he has twice been mugged, and on one occasion badly beaten.

The actor playing Kyle has an open, vulnerable manner, and he is prepared from the start to engage with the dilemma between his fear and his compassion. However, the actor playing Michael finds it hard not to give us the 'drug dealer' character, with all its bravado and swagger. As a result, his 'fear' is not believable, and neither we nor his fellow actor can respond to it. The actor playing Kyle has learned to be honest in his observations:

KYLE   You're not really scared.

MICHAEL   I'm not really scared??!

KYLE   You're not really scared.

MICHAEL   They're gonna kill me, man!

KYLE   They're gonna kill you?

MICHAEL   They're gonna kill me!!

KYLE   No one's going to kill you.

MICHAEL   No one's going to kill me?

We have to stop, because the basic premise of the scene simply isn't there, namely the genuine belief of the actors in the given circumstances, starting with the actor playing Michael. To help him, we send him up to the top of the building (eight flights of stairs), with the instruction to sprint down to the studio as if there is an unseen pursuer always keeping just out of sight behind him, and bang on the door. I also remind the actor playing Michael that, from the moment he enters the room and engages with Kyle, the issue is not with the pursuer – he can't in this moment do anything about him – but with Kyle. Michael's life depends not on the person out to kill him, but on whether Kyle will allow him to stay.

The second time, the actor playing Michael is genuinely out of breath, and something about the dynamic of his entrance, which really startles Kyle, takes us straight onto the right energy level:

KYLE   You burst in through my door.

MICHAEL   I burst in through your door.

KYLE   You just barged in.

MICHAEL   I just barged in.

KYLE   You went right over to the wall.

MICHAEL   I went right over to the wall... They want to kill me!

KYLE   They want to kill you?

MICHAEL   The dealers – they want to kill me!

KYLE   The dealers want to kill you??

MICHAEL   You don't believe me.

KYLE   I don't believe you... You're shaking.

MICHAEL   I'm shaking.

KYLE   You're scared.

MICHAEL   You're worried.

KYLE   I'm worried.

MICHAEL   You looked at the door.

KYLE   I looked at the door.

MICHAEL   You're scared they saw me come in.

KYLE   I'm scared they saw you come in.

MICHAEL   You're scared they'll get you too.

KYLE   I'm scared they'll get me too... Get out of my flat.

MICHAEL   Get out of your flat??

KYLE   Get out of my fucking flat!

MICHAEL   You shouted.

KYLE   I shouted.

MICHAEL   You know my mum.

KYLE   I know your mum.

MICHAEL   You don't know what to do.

KYLE   I don't know what to do!

MICHAEL   You don't know what to do.

KYLE   You brought your mess into my home.

MICHAEL   I brought my mess into your home.

At this point, having had us on the edge of our seats, the actor playing Michael suddenly stops trusting either the repetition or the relationship. It is as if he senses that they have reached a turning point in the scene, and can't resist putting a 'bid' on his last response. Instead of an open and vulnerable admission of Kyle's statement, Michael reverts to a manipulative fake contrition, with submissive gestures borrowed from action comics.

This is a fine example of what I call 'the director in the head' – the self-observational part of the brain that can plague actors by pulling them out of the moment, making them contrive and present rather than live a key moment. Because this moment stood in such stark contrast to the rest of the improvisation, the group could see the effect of such a choice with startling clarity. Interestingly, although the gestures of the fake moment did smack of cliché, it was not the gestures themselves that were problematic, but their lack of connection to the rest of the scene, and to the actor's actual emotional journey.

'Trusting the moment' is one of the most important precepts for the actor. The process of exploration and discovery through improvisation and rehearsal is of little value if you try to stay in conscious artistic control throughout. Even in performance, when much of the physical journey of a scene has been decided upon and embedded, you need to trust that the interaction with your scene partner is still the determinant of your choices within each moment.

If you try to reproduce a previous successful performance, you will always come unstuck, because while you may be able to fix and fine-tune your own gestures and delivery, you cannot control what other actors do. It makes sense, therefore, for you to let your scene partner bring your performance out of you – to give them control.

Like many actors, you probably worry that relinquishing control in this way will put you at risk of 'messing up' – failing to deliver the right line or do the right move, or just not taking the scene in the direction it needs to go.

A trainee actor was once asked how she travelled to class that morning. She replied that she came by Tube, and it was soon established that she did the same journey every weekday morning, and had done so for the past eighteen months since she joined the course. She was then asked whether she had to think about the journey – where to find the station, how to operate the ticket barrier, which train to get on, et cetera. She said no, she thought about other things, such as the day's work or her personal preoccupations, or even the people on the train.

It is quite possible for you to learn to follow a pre-established pattern of actions quite faultlessly while keeping your attention on something else. Even if you don't give the details of your journey the slightest conscious thought, you don't get lost, because the pattern of the journey is embedded in your brain. But there is still a relationship between the routine of the journey and the immediacy of the moment, because the two are interlaced and mutually affective within the totality of the living person.

So it is with acting. The lines, the moves, the stage business, are learned and delivered accurately and in the right order, but they are not *reproduced*, because, as with the actor's journey to school, there will always be subtle differences between each journey and, as a result, subtle differences in your responses. Thus each journey, although identical in so many ways, is in other senses unique.

Even the outline of each character's emotional journey, having been teased out interactively, can be accurately preserved in performance, again without removing your capacity for spontaneous response. You can know *what* you are going to do, but not know *how* you will choose to do it in the moment, nor *why* you will make that particular choice. Each performance has the potential to be unique and, provided that uniqueness is born out of uncensored interaction, to be real.

The Knock on the Door exercise will help you understand both in mind and in body the difference between uncensored organic work and work which is contrived. Having once had the heady experience of letting your scene partner determine your performance, you will not want to return to the painful process of forcing and demonstrating.

Therein lies the power of repetition. You have probably at some point done free improvisation around a given scenario, but unless you have trained yourself always to look to the other actor for inspiration and direction, it is likely that you responded more readily to your own inner instructions than to the reality of what was in front of you. Repetition, if you are honest with it, forces you to keep changing direction, accommodating, adapting, shifting your energies, in ways that make you both believable and exciting to watch. It can also help you access answers and solutions that lie just beyond the reach of your conscious enquiring mind.

9
Playing with Text

'You keep talking… not on the basis of what she's doing, but in order to perform'

Playing with Text

You now have to make a significant shift, which is to apply your skills to pre-scripted text rather than improvisations. The improvisation work that makes up the early part of Meisner training is largely a preparation for the moment when you will start working with text. For the mainstream professional actor, whether in classical theatre or contemporary television, the text is central to the work, and it is the actor's job to fulfil the demands of the text, bringing to life both the words and the physical world suggested by the playwright.

Almost all lines of dramatic text are a response to something – usually another line of text and the accompanying non-verbal signals. This means that, for the actor, the speaking of every line should be a choice made in the moment. The words themselves may be fixed, but if you allow yourself in each moment to *choose* to speak them, then you can almost believe that you have chosen the words as well as the manner of delivery, since in inflecting the words within the context of each moment, you also gain ownership of them – and, what is more, you feel the need to speak them. You speak those words because those are what you have – they are your only way of changing and improving the situation you find yourself in.

The next three chapters contain examples of different kinds of text and some of the problems that can arise for actors as they attempt to make scripts and characters their own. There are also examples of exercises that I have used on these and other occasions to help actors find firstly a personal/emotional connection with the character and situation, and secondly a genuine, responsive relationship with other actors in pursuit of an objective. None of these exercises represents a complete rehearsal process, and at points along the way I have drawn attention to other kinds of process work and preparation which I believe actors need to undertake in order to achieve these goals.

Meisner believed that if an actor is emotionally 'prepared' for a scene – i.e. able to connect emotionally with the character's situation – then the combination of that raw yet specific emotion with the reactions of the other characters will allow the text to emerge spontaneously. He likened the flow of emotion to a river, and the text to a canoe carried on its current.

As in the Knock on the Door exercise, Meisner's main preoccupation when working on text was to enable his actors to find the 'as if' that would connect them to the emotional life of a character within a story. Having found this connection, an actor could then practise the interactive skills learned in repetition work, and by a continual process of reading and responding to other actors, a scene would begin to emerge.

This sounds very simple and obvious, but it is astonishing how few actors understand the importance of allowing the text to be spoken in direct response to an emotional impulse arising from a real interaction. All too many actors seek to inflect the text according to their own personal interpretation, regardless of what is actually happening in the space, as if scared that a response genuinely derived from the moment will be in some way 'incorrect'. This desire to control the text allows the audience to understand a scene intellectually, but not to follow the emotional journey of the characters, which makes the experience empty and dull.

First Approaches

Some of the preparatory exercises described in the remainder of this book do not derive directly from Meisner, but it would seem futile to be purist or exclusive about this. Meisner himself simply wanted his actors to be both informed about and emotionally in touch with the key aspects of their fictional situation so that they could respond to other actors appropriately. My view is that you cannot successfully transfer skills from the repetition exercises to work on text without a secure and efficient process for acquiring a solid understanding of the character's background and situation, including the conditioning forces that affect his choices and behaviour. The ability to respond in an organic and uncensored way to another actor is an invaluable skill, but if you are responding without context then arguably you are responding as someone in your own physical and emotional circumstances rather than as someone in the character's circumstances – which by logical extension means that the messages the other actor receives in rehearsal will be misleading and incoherent.

Before you start applying a systematic text-preparation process, you will find it beneficial to spend some time just 'playing' with text, in order to try out the skills you have acquired during the repetition exercises in a way that feels unburdened with the responsibilities to the playwright, which you might feel in a later rehearsal or a performance. The first time you apply Meisner Technique to text is a crucial point in your journey, because you may previously have been accustomed to thinking about text as something that has to be delivered in the 'right' way, whereas in Meisner there is no 'right' way – there is only the truth of the moment. To play with the text before you know very much about the character places the moment of doing at the centre of your work, and means that the process of building the character starts with your reactions to the other character.

Ideally, you should start with short contemporary duologues, which in the first instance allow you to apply preparation techniques in a simplified and straightforward way. You may need to read the rest of the play in order to extract key background facts and information, but for the most part you should remain focused on the chosen extract itself.

To begin with, you learn the words accurately and thoroughly, but try not to make fixed choices about how to deliver them. This will stop the text from weighing you down as you struggle to remember a line. You should then do the following preparatory work, so that you can understand just enough about character and context to be able to make sense of the scene, and to jolt you from your own world and habits into the fictional world of the play.

The Lists

What your character does during the scene: This is a simple list, which includes the facts from the text and also strong probabilities – e.g. if your character is sitting at a breakfast table they are probably eating breakfast. The list usually includes all the stated or implied physical actions, plus a simple summary of the dialogue, such as 'She talks to her daughter about the noise she made coming in the previous night.'

What your character knows at the start of the scene: This contains all the relevant facts that contextualise the scene. It contains everything from the background facts to the specifics of this particular time and place. The text will give you almost all of this, and whatever it doesn't state, you can either work out for yourself (such as the approximate age of your character) or leave aside for the moment. To be clear about what your character knows at the point where the scene starts is essential preparation, because this can hugely affect your character's reactions to events in the scene.

Objective(s): This is your character's 'want' during the scene. In order to play productively with a text, it is necessary to identify a 'working' objective, and to spend a little time thinking around that objective, so that it becomes a story you can relate to. Identifying the objective will usually also reveal which character in the duologue is the scene-driver – in other words, who has the stronger objective.

Obstacle(s): Only by knowing what, in your scene partner, is the obstacle or resistance to the fulfilment of your objective, can you be really interested in her. Once you start to play the scene, you will experience the obstacle in her reaction to you, but even before that you need to understand something of your character's *attitude* towards the other character. From the text you can glean something of the expectation each character has of the other, which will set the tone of the scene.

Armed with this relatively simple set of facts and choices, you can start to work on the text, and to make discoveries based on moments of connection and realisation in the moment, rather than an intellectual analysis.

To ease you in to the practical task of delivering text as a Meisner actor, I would probably ask you to begin with an exercise I call Text Repetition. Again, this is not strictly a Meisner exercise, but it is a useful stepping stone from improvised repetition into text.

Text Repetition

Before you start, you need to look at your own character's lines within the scene and break up each line into *thoughts*. The extent of one thought is hard to define – in some text a single thought can last three or four lines – but for the purposes of repetition it might be better to call a thought a 'bite-sized chunk' of text, which is easily repeatable.

Many of a character's speeches will be single-thought lines, but where a character has a slightly longer speech, this speech may contain two or more separate thoughts. New thoughts are generally stimulated during the speaking of the previous thought, and very often will be a direct reaction to something the other character does in that moment.

You will also need to learn your character's lines, trying to avoid making fixed choices about how they should be delivered. This does not mean that you learn them as a flat monotone (a common mistake) but that you experiment with pitch, volume and intonation as you learn so that no single interpretation emerges. What you should *not* do at this stage is rehearse or try out the scene with your scene partner.

Finally, it is important to spend a little time on emotional preparation and a little more time on physical preparation, so that you can start the scene with the appropriate energy level. You can do this with your partner in much the same way that you prepared for the Knock on the Door scenes in the previous chapters.

The actor with the first line of the scene then speaks his or her first thought, and the other actor repeats it back, again with the 'I' and 'you' reversed. This thought then goes back and forth like an improvised repetition line, until the actor with the *next* thought has the impulse to speak that line. This thought is then repeated in the same way, and so it goes on.

It is essential that the repeated lines are not treated differently from the original text. They should be as much a part of the interaction as the learned lines. Theoretically, it should be impossible for anyone observing, unless they know the play well, to distinguish the repeated lines from the originals.

The example below is taken from Scene Two of Stella Feehily's play *Duck*. The characters are Val (late thirties) and her daughter, Sophie (late teens). It is Sunday morning in the kitchen at their home. The previous night Sophie and her friend Cat had been in a fight with two boys. Sophie has cut both of the boys with a broken bottle and has been punched in the face. This morning she is feeling hungover and battered. Although unaware of the precise events of the previous night, Val is anxious and disapproving of Sophie's lifestyle and friendships, and worries she will drop out of college. Sophie has a plaster on her nose.

The opening exchange is written as follows:

VAL   Thought a pack of elephants had arrived at
          six o'clock this morning.

SOPHIE   Sorry, thought we were being quiet.

VAL   Well you know what thought did.

SOPHIE   No what?

VAL   What do you mean 'No what?'
          Are you being smart wench?

SOPHIE   No.

VAL   You said you'd be back by three.

With Text Repetition the scene might go more like this (the lines in italics are the repeated lines):

VAL   Thought a pack of elephants had arrived at
          six o'clock this morning.

SOPHIE   *You thought a pack of elephants had arrived...*

VAL	*I thought a pack of elephants had arrived…*
SOPHIE	Sorry, thought we were being quiet.
VAL	*You thought you were being quiet??!*
SOPHIE	*We thought we were being quiet.*
VAL	Well you know what thought did.
SOPHIE	*I know what thought did?*
VAL	*You know what thought did.*
SOPHIE	No what?
VAL	*No what??*
SOPHIE	*No what?*
VAL	What do you mean 'No what?'
SOPHIE	*What do I mean?*
VAL	*What do you mean?*
SOPHIE	*What do I mean?*
VAL	Are you being smart wench?
SOPHIE	*Am I being smart?*
VAL	*Are you being smart?*
SOPHIE	No.
VAL	*No?*
SOPHIE	*No.*
VAL	You said you'd be back by three.

It is worth observing at this point that, in Text Repetition, you should never be dogged or literal about repeating every word or syllable of what you hear. Very often, in order to keep a line sounding natural and credible, it is necessary to add or leave out words. It is only the main body of the thought that needs to be repeated verbatim.

Text Repetition compels you to listen and respond, because if you don't, you will quickly end up with something that sounds forced, mechanical and stilted. There is no time to think, so the responses have to emerge, in the context of the relationship, the circumstances and the objective, as spontaneously as an improvised line. Similarly, the choice to shift on to the next thought should be an organic moment in which the character has the *need* to speak the line rather than you the actor feeling she ought to!

When you play a scene that you and your partner have both studied and learned, it is entirely possible for you to construct between you a way of delivering all the lines which is coherent, comprehensible and even emotional, but which has no real truth in the moment. It is probable that some actors have spent whole careers dealing in such constructions, often with such skill that we hardly know why we are fundamentally unconvinced by the work. Text Repetition can unpick the safe and fixed choices an actor has made, and turn the text, which the actor has thought of as fixed, into something living, flexible and infinitely variable.

It can take a while, even after months of Meisner training, to join up the two seemingly irreconcilable processes of delivering a line from someone else's play and being a living breathing human in the moment. For this reason it is a good idea to start each rehearsal with fifteen to twenty minutes of Text Repetition. The idea is that by developing the skill of playing with the text, without paraphrasing or making up your own lines, you can start to forge a new and different relationship with scripted plays.

By the time you begin working on the scenes as written, you should have a sense of the scene as something alive and fluid rather than fixed and unwieldy. It is important for you to feel that you are *choosing* in the moment to speak a line, possibly because you are picking up from the Text Repetition an awareness that there are other things you could say or other moments at which you could say that line. This gives the spoken text an edge and makes an audience want to listen.

The moment you try to work without repetition, you will probably have an initial sense of disappointment. Once you lose the repetition, you may also seem to lose something of the pulse of its back-and-forth rhythm, which can make you less able to stay connected and less able to speak in direct response to your partner. For this reason it is better not to abandon the repetition too suddenly, but to let it go gradually.

The scene from *Duck* has quite a conventional 'arc', in that it builds to a climax of anger and conflict, followed by a post-climactic section in which mother and daughter struggle to find a point of contact but are unable to do so because of the simmering disapproval and resentment still in the way. As in some of the Knock on the Door scenes, you may feel pressure to deliver that arc and to take the scene on its journey, rather than letting it take you. You may feel you have to generate emotion at certain points where the text demands it, and this will make you focus on that task rather than on the relationship, as though you simply can't trust the interaction itself to take you where you need to go.

For this reason it is best to proceed via a 'halfway house' form of Text Repetition, in which you repeat not whole lines, but the opening few syllables. In other words, you *start* to repeat, and are either interrupted or interrupt yourself with your own line, as follows:

VAL	Thought a pack of elephants had arrived at six o'clock this morning.
SOPHIE	*You thought a...* Sorry, thought we were being quiet.
VAL	*You thought you were...* Well you know what thought did.
SOPHIE	*I...* No what?
VAL	What do you mean 'No what?'
SOPHIE	*What do I..?*
VAL	Are you being smart wench?

SOPHIE   *Am I being... No.*

VAL   You said you'd be back by three.

The point at which the interruption happens is up to you. It should be a spontaneous choice, not decided beforehand.

This version of Text Repetition tends to be very fast-paced, and this will stop you from 'planning' your way through the scene or thinking 'actor thoughts'. Once again you are dependent on the other actor for your next line, and once again you have to inhabit the verbal landscape rather than sculpting it. Between the repetition and the retort there is a point of imbalance which is an intensely real moment.

The element of uncertainty for the actor within that real moment equates to the character's experience of living the moment for the first time. We all understand the difference between a ritualised dialogue and one that is happening for the first and only time. Ritualised dialogues take place in shops, registry offices and other places of work and officialdom. In such contexts the dialogue is probably not being used to secure a particular outcome – we already know the outcome – so our use of language will often be contrived and inorganic, and much of our effort may be focused on trying to make oft-pronounced phrases *sound* new and exciting, usually without success. All too many actors do much the same, inflecting their lines with considerably more skill but no more spontaneity than the average shop assistant reciting sales patter.

You have to find ways of making your text not just *seem* alive but actually *be* alive in the space, without the help and support of the repetition. In the earlier Meisner exercises, the idea was to reprogramme your habits in order to allow the other actor to be the determinant of your next line. On text, of course, once we have removed the elements of repetition, your partner cannot actually determine *which* words you will speak, but she can still have a huge influence on *how* and *why* they are spoken.

Example 1

I ask two actors to play the scene from *Duck* with this in mind. They are instructed not to inflect their lines according to any prior interpretation, but to breathe in the presence of the other actor and speak in response to what they hear.

The first time they do this, we lose most of the scene's clearly contentious atmosphere. Sophie comes across as much more submissive and her mother more caring, as a result of the actors becoming sensitised to one another. This is perhaps not how the scene should ultimately be played, but the actors have at least found a connection and are starting to work off one another. Observing it, we believe that this is a real conversation, and that each actor is affecting the responses of the other. We can work with this, because its starting point is the reality of the relationship, not either actor's preconceived idea of how the scene should be played.

Now we have to revisit the given circumstances and do some further emotional preparation to ensure that the actors can start the scene from the right place. We remind ourselves of Val's fear that her daughter will drop out of college and end up working in a supermarket or getting pregnant. Val is also very annoyed about the noise the previous night. We remind ourselves that Sophie has a bad hangover and her nose is very painful. We talk about the possibility that Val has constantly tried to talk to Sophie about her behaviour and her future, and that Sophie finds this intolerable.

Another useful tool which the actors can use at this point is the 'silent étude'. This can be defined as the playing of the action of the scene without using words. The purpose of études in early rehearsal is two-fold. Firstly, they recreate the idea of the 'objective and activity', so that you and your scene partner have a clear sense of the scene-driver's strong objective and the other character's (initially) weaker objective. Secondly, études also help you to gain a fuller sense of space and place. When you start working within a fictional world you need to know what the space looks and feels like, because this information forms a key part of your given circumstances. If your body comprehends the fictional space then your impulses will translate much more freely into physical gesture and physical action.

Example 1 continued

The actors do a silent étude in which Sophie, complete with hangover and injured nose, tries to make herself some breakfast while Val watches her. Without text but with objectives, the atmosphere builds. At various points, Sophie has to stop what she is doing and nurse her aching head. Various questions flicker across Val's face.

Eventually, the actors play the scene as written, and this time we get both the atmosphere and the connection. Both actors become immersed in the relationship and the given circumstances. We can see that Sophie is desperate not to get into a conflict because she feels too unwell to deal with it, while Val needs answers and reassurance. For the first time the scene is driven from the relationship and the embodied objectives, not from the actors' manufactured vocal choices. The text is now really afloat on the action of the scene.

The scene is so convincing and seems so genuine that immediately a question arises from the group, which is why Sophie, who is clearly uncomfortable with the questions, does not leave the kitchen and go to her room. We consult the back-stories and decide that despite her ability to fight off male aggression in the street, she is genuinely afraid of her mother, who is often verbally aggressive and occasionally violent (there is evidence for this in the text). We add to the backstory one or two incidents from Sophie's childhood and adolescence in which Val has beaten her quite badly. We then explore this by playing the scene with a strong undercurrent of suppressed physical violence from Val, and a corresponding wariness from Sophie. This creates a strong physical dynamic which further builds the spatial relationship and the sense of uncertainty. It also builds the emotional subtext, because, as the text suggests, for both characters the violence is linked to disillusion and disappointment in one another. Again, this is not a finished version of the scene, but it forms part of the exploratory layering so essential to a good rehearsal process.

What you can learn from this, among other things, is that a scene can only move forward in rehearsal if the actors are connecting with each other, because only within the truth of the reactive moment can we see the impulses in the body that tell us how the scene should develop, or, as in the example above, what adjustments need to be made to the actor's 'inner landscape' in order for the scene to make sense.

A scene which has been explored and rehearsed in this way will both retain its spontaneity in performance, and have an internal logic. In the course of rehearsal you will have addressed any contradictions or logical flaws and found a through-line which makes sense and the actors are able to inhabit.

You may still ask: 'What if the other actor simply doesn't give me what I need to play the scene?' The only possible answer to this is that whatever happens it cannot be worse than fake, inorganic acting. If you are genuinely and truthfully responding to another actor, and doing so within the given circumstances of the play, a scene may not immediately play out as you want it to, but at least you can start the journey.

There is an important lesson to be learned here, which is that you should never 'endgame' in your work by trying to deliver the idea of a scene you have in your head. If a scene doesn't appear to be going in the right direction despite the actors responding truthfully to each other, then this is merely an indicator that you have not built the inner life of the characters sufficiently and are therefore not responding from the right place. This is not a bad thing, because it is also an indicator of precisely what aspect of the character you haven't attended to, and what additional work needs to be done in order to make the scene work. Much of the next chapter is devoted to exercises and techniques for doing that work.

Playing with the text is useful not just for actors making the transition from repetition to text, but for any actors starting to work on a play, whether in an investigative workshop or at the start of rehearsal. You need always to remember that the effortless responsiveness you can achieve when you know only a few basic facts about the character and context is something you need to maintain all through rehearsal and performance, even when you have delved much more deeply into the background, history and emotional inner life of the character. You can never play context – you can only play *from* context. This means that, even after weeks of rehearsal, it will still be the other character who is the principal determinant of what you feel, think and do.

10

Exploring Character

'What you read in the book is only the merest indication of what you have to do when you really act the part'

Exploring Character

In the last chapter you were introduced to a few of the preparatory exercises through which an actor extracts information from the text and starts little by little to live in the character's world. This chapter offers you many more techniques to enable you to delve further into the physical and emotional life of your character, so that you can start to genuinely experience the interactive moment in the space from the character's point of view.

No matter what kind of text you are working from, Meisner's fundamental principle – that the *other actor* is the determinant of *your* responses and behaviour – still always applies. Your repetition work is merely the training of the metaphorical 'muscle' that allows you to stay open rather than closed throughout a scene. What this means is that your preparation for a role must be meticulous, because you need to be confident that you are responding from within the *character's* circumstances and emotional landscape, and not your own.

Exploring the Character's World

To serve the text, especially if the play is set in a different country or era from your own, you will need to be starting to work not as yourself in your own circumstances early on, but from within an imagined world, so that every spontaneous response you make in the space is heavily influenced (though not predetermined) by the circumstances and immediate needs of your character within that world. To that end, you need to have a clear and systematic process for extracting, fleshing out and embodying the information the text offers.

Different plays and characters require different levels of investigation, and there are many approaches (most derived from Stanislavsky) that can assist you in achieving an embodied understanding of the text. There are no precise rules, because every character is different and every actor is different, but you need in every case to find a balance between working with too much information and too little. You cannot bring every detail of the character's life onstage with you, but by the time you perform a role you need to have responded emotionally to the key events within the character's story and have found within yourself a strong empathy – not just with *what* the character feels but *how* that feeling is experienced and expressed.

Before embarking on this work, you need to remind yourself to approach playscripts in a workmanlike and systematic way. When you read a play you may be intrigued and moved, and you may respond to it with all kinds of creative ideas. For the professional actor, this is only a starting point for an exploratory journey which may take you in many directions. Your first impressions and ideas may be useful or even inspired, and you may come back to them in the course of rehearsal, but you must be prepared in the first instance to put them to one side and consider many other possibilities. If you do not, then your rehearsal process will be a frustrating series of attempts to deliver a preconceived idea, rather than a genuine exploration.

For the actor, the text of a play is a treasure chest of clues and information. Sometimes a lot of the information you need to know about your character and the world of the play will only be hinted at rather than explicitly stated. Some plays scatter information through the text like puzzle pieces for you to gather up and put together. The first part of your job is to study the text, find out the relevant hard facts, and identify other possible facts that seem to fit. There are different methods available for listing and recording this information, including the 'lists' described in the last chapter, but text study should never be allowed to become mechanical or turn into a pointless paper exercise. Your principal aim is to emerge from this period of study with as much clarity as possible about the age, gender, lifestyle, location, class, education, politics, occupation, back-story, knowledge, relationships and current situation of the character, plus significant information as appropriate about other characters and the wider location.

Living the Context

Some facts in a play open up questions rather than providing answers. If you are in Chekhov's *The Cherry Orchard* playing Yasha, a valet in a provincial Russian mansion around 1900, your first investigation should be into the nature and duties of this role, using whatever accurate information sources you can find, because you will find it hard to explore a character in the acting space if you haven't understood that character's world.

It is often said that drama is 'interrupted ritual' – in other words, that most plays are about the exceptional event or series of events within an otherwise uneventful or routine existence. In order for the actor to live the interruption as the character, he or she must first have lived the routine. It is not enough to *know* what a valet does – you also need to have lived as a valet, if only for an hour or two within an étude or improvisation, so that you understand at least something about what it feels like to live that life, and how you personally respond to its sensations. Of course, it is not always easy to reproduce your character's everyday experience, but you can usually find a way to explore certain detailed aspects of it, and this is often sufficient to stimulate the sensory imagination.

Reading Between the Lines

You will also have to spend time exploring the significant events that do not take place onstage, but are mentioned or indicated in the text, and are clearly influential within the drama. Past scenes or encounters may be referred to in a play's dialogue, and there may also be events which take place *between* the scenes or acts of a play. It is essential that you investigate these and preferably take the time to improvise and play out the missing scenes with other actors. In this way you can enter the space not just knowing the backstory, but with the experience of living it in your memory.

Sometimes it is also necessary to improvise scenes that are not even mentioned in the text, in order to clarify for yourself a particular relationship with another character that the play does not explore. Provided you do not stray from the facts within the text, nor introduce unnecessary plot elements, these improvised scenes can be an excellent way to start making the character your own, because they bring together the established facts (including those of the wider world in which the play takes place), your own creative sense of the character and the active exploratory process with other members of the cast. The actor playing Yasha might decide, for instance, to improvise a scene with his peasant mother (a character who never appears in the play but who, the text tells us, waits outside hoping to see her son). Yasha is clearly ashamed of his mother and refuses to see her, so the improvisation might centre on the mother's mixture of pride in her son's advancement and hurt bewilderment at his rejection of the family. This would provide the actor with clear factual and emotional reference points, giving him a clear sense of emotional dilemma, and adding resonance and meaning to lines of text which might otherwise be thrown away.

The point here is that you cannot get very far with a role until you have really worked to flesh out the information in the text in order to gain a fuller and deeper understanding of the character's given circumstances within the world of the play. Every signal conveyed and interpreted within a human interaction finds its meaning through the context, and only by understanding that context as fully as possible can we start the kind of meaningful exploration that leads to significant discoveries.

Example 1

In James Baldwin's play *Blues for Mister Charlie*, set in the Deep South of the United States in the late 1950s, there are many characters of whom we get only a glimpse in one or two scenes. The play is about the racial struggle between black and white communities, and the dialogue centres on the murder of a young black man by a white shopkeeper. For this reason, most of the characters are defined largely by their political stance on the central issue. Yet for an actor to play even a minor character within this play purely on that basis would be to make the character, and therefore the production, very two-dimensional. Baldwin's writing is anything but simplistic; he penetrates the inner lives of both black and white characters, seeking to shine a light onto the psychological and emotional straitjackets in which the characters live. If you were cast as a minor character in this play, it would be your job, therefore, to pick up the very few clues offered in the text and flesh out the character – not in a random way, but in a way that offers both you and your audience an insight into both the world of the play and the individual world of your character.

Act Two, Scene One of the play is set in 'White-town' on a Sunday morning. Rather than going to church, a group of white people, including the minister, have gathered at the house of Lyle Britten, the shopkeeper accused of murder and about to be arrested. Ostensibly they are there to offer their support; in reality it is almost the opposite. They rely on Lyle's tough, outspoken approach to racial segregation to reassure them and shore up their own position. Beneath their message of support is a veiled warning to him not to weaken or waver.

The various characters in the scene reveal themselves through small clues. The character of George, for instance, has few lines, and there is virtually no information about him, but if you look closely, you see that there are two things which preoccupy him. The first is encouraging the rest of the company to drink a toast in hard liquor (despite the time of day):

> GEORGE   I'd propose a toast to them, if it wasn't so
> early on a Sunday, and if the Reverend wasn't
> here.

The second is bemoaning the passing of the 'old' arrangement of complete segregation between black and white communities. In particular he warns against what he calls 'them yellow niggers' – people of mixed race.

> GEORGE   You might be able to scare a black nigger, but
> you can't do nothing with a yellow nigger.

From these clues it is not hard to extrapolate that George is most probably an ageing alcoholic whose only sources of self-esteem are his 'whiteness' and his ability to bully and intimidate black people. There is no evidence that he is married, and no mention of his job, so you could also conclude that he is quite an unsuccessful person, who sits near the bottom of the white community's 'pecking order'. Mixed-race 'yellow niggers' represent for him a dangerous erosion of the clear divide between white and black from which he draws his self-esteem.

As an actor playing George, you now have a challenge. It probably isn't hard to play George as a racist stereotype, in which the caricature is so extreme that both actor and audience can just laugh at it from a distance, yet to do so would not serve the play. For George to work as a character, he has to reflect – albeit in quite an extreme way – the insecurity and fear within white people then and now, which even in the twenty-first century continues to hinder our progress towards full racial equality. Your job as the actor, therefore, is to get inside George, to live in his world and to see life through his eyes, however repugnant he may initially seem to be.

Creative improvisation is probably the best way for you to start to *live* as George. Your improvisations can explore and flesh out the clues and signposts the text provides. For example, you could do an improvisation in which George has drunk too much and collapsed in the street, and is helped home by a kindly black man, or is refused service in a black bar because he is too drunk. You could also do an improvisation set in Lyle's store, in which Lyle serves a black customer before George, because the black customer has money and George is asking for credit. Improvisations of this kind explore the way in which George's status is increasingly threatened as the black community begins to acquire education, money and civil rights.

Through improvisation, you do not have to try and embrace racist thoughts and attitudes you find distasteful – you merely have to *experience* what it feels like to be at the bottom of the social order. From that place it is all too easy to clutch at any opportunity to raise your own status and put someone else below you. Neither you nor your audience will have any difficulty recognising that George and his behaviours are just an extreme version of how we all behave or are tempted to behave, and that, I believe, is one of Baldwin's principal intentions in writing the play.

Maintaining Spontaneity

Having said all of this, it is terribly important not to make any decisions in advance about how to play a scene, beyond the specific instructions of the playwright – and even those can sometimes be challenged. Meisner himself was deeply opposed to most stage directions – especially those which hinted at a character's feelings – and often asked his actors to cross out the directions in their scripts, leaving only the text itself. You cannot decide beforehand what your character will feel, nor can you decide exactly how a line of text will be spoken, before you get it onto its feet. In the first instance, your study should confine itself to extracting all the information the text has to offer, on character, on situation, on relationships. You also need to ensure that you understand all the words and references in the dialogue, even if these are just figures of speech or metaphors, because part of the process of rehearsal is to take as much ownership as possible of the character's mode of speaking, knowledge base and past experience.

Actors who decide before the first rehearsal how they are going to play a scene might as well not bother rehearsing it at all. Some actors seem to think they will please the director by not only learning their lines but also creating something akin to a polished performance by day one. Few directors like this. Most will want to direct by observing the raw material that emerges from a much more open and exploratory interaction and shaping this gradually into a presentable form.

Making a Connection

Getting the information out of the text and asking yourself questions about your character is an essential starting point, but you should not make the mistake of thinking that it is enough just to know these things. Facts on their own will not allow you to respond in the moment as the character. You have to go on an exploratory journey, the aim of which is to use those facts to create within yourself an emotional inner life. Without that 'inner' in place you will never be able to trust that the interactions in the space will remain true to the character and the play.

There are many exercises you can undertake to help you begin to think and feel as the character. You will probably find that some of these work better for you than others, because all actors are stimulated by different things:

- Fleshing the known facts and the character's statements about him or herself within the text into a coherent but not overdetailed backstory, paying particular attention to a very few *key events* in the past that might have had a particular influence on the character's behaviour during the scene in question.
- Improvising some or all of these events.
- Writing character diary entries.
- Wearing clothes and, where possible, visiting places appropriate to the character.
- Creating the character's own space and possessions (whether or not any scene in the play actually takes place in that room), and existing alone within that space for periods of fifteen to thirty minutes at a time.
- Making decisions about the location/room layout where a scene takes place (i.e. decor, contents), and your character's relationship and reaction to the space.
- Walking, sitting, sensing in that space.

Forging a connection with the character by living in the character's own world can take time, but it cannot be rushed. In seeking to achieve an empathy that is mental, physical and emotional, you are committing yourself to a process of laying down new memories in your mind and body, so that your responses in the moment can be effortlessly informed by those memories rather than forced and contrived.

A Point of View

One of the most significant things Meisner said about the actor speaking text is that he or she needs a *point of view*, which reveals itself in the inflection of each line of text he or she speaks. The 'point of view' is a very useful concept for you to keep in mind, because it stops you ignoring the fact that your job as an actor is to respond to other actors from the emotional and cognitive standpoint of your character. The 'point of view' encapsulates, in one phrase, the whole range of concepts you have learned to work with, including given circumstances, character objective and the 'emotional inner landscape'. It therefore informs and shapes your attitude and response to each moment in the text.

The 'point of view' works on a number of levels. On one level it is simply the character's opinion, or attitude, towards a moment within the text, based on the character's current circumstances and immediate situation. Sometimes this 'point of view' is obvious and explicit – at other times it needs to be discovered and laid down within the subtext, as in the following example.

Example 2

In Act Two of Chekhov's *Three Sisters*, the character of Natasha dismisses the musicians who are due to play at the Prozorov house at carnival time. She claims that this is because her young child is ill, but at the end of the act, when everyone has gone home in disappointment, Natasha slips out for a troika ride with her admirer Protopopov, thereby revealing her real motive in cancelling the party – a motive she obviously cannot afford to reveal to any of the other characters.

If the actor playing Natasha knows and works with this objective from the start of the act, then she will have a clear 'point of view' which will affect all her interactions. The audience may not know exactly what is going on until the end of the act, but they will understand that Natasha's responses to other characters are being influenced by a strong inner motivation.

On another level, the 'point of view' can be a much deeper awareness of the character's emotional drivers, which connects each moment in the dialogue with the character's 'inner emotional landscape'. This inner landscape can be described as the sum total of the character's significant memories and past experiences, not necessarily as they actually happened, but as the character understands and feels them. These memories and images do not lie passively in the actor's imagination, but interact with the character's present, generating desires, objectives, ways of seeing the world, and impulses, all of which influence the character's responses in the moment.

Example 3

The character of Olga in *Three Sisters* is obsessed with the idea of returning to Moscow, where she grew up. She hates the isolated and uncultured provincial town where she now lives and works. At the start of Act One, the anniversary of her father's death, Olga relives the day of his funeral and reaffirms her determination to go back to Moscow, a place which she glamorises in her imagination. From that point on, everyone who enters the room stirs something within Olga's inner landscape.

When Lieutenant-Colonel Vershinin, newly arrived in the town, starts to speak about his own life in Moscow a few minutes later, he creates a very different picture from that in Olga's imagination:

> VERSHININ I used to walk from Nemetsky Street to the
> old Krasny Barracks. There's a gloomy-
> looking bridge on the way, with the water
> roaring underneath it. You could feel quite
> depressed, if you were on your own.

It is clear from the awkward pause that follows that neither Olga nor her sisters can quite deal with the idea of being depressed in Moscow. Such a notion sits uncomfortably, even dangerously, with their hopes. Olga in particular sees Vershinin as a little piece of Moscow. She expects him to reinforce and validate all her dreams, not shatter them. Olga's reaction to this line needs to be clear and palpable even in her silence. Yet it is only when the actor has built Olga's 'inner landscape' that we can understand this as both a deeply resonant, and a purely reactive, moment.

The Need

From the inner landscape arises what Meisner called the 'need' of the character. The need equates to a kind of personal super-objective – in other words, it is the fundamental problem or 'black hole' at the centre of a character's life. This is not the same as the objective; but all objectives, large and small, flow from it.

The need can be expressed simply, but it is rarely simple in itself, because it is simultaneously a literal desire, an emotional state and a sensual landscape. In other words, it inhabits the mind, the emotions and the body. The need is not a fixed concept, and different actors may discover different needs for the same character.

The best way of identifying the 'need' of a character is to make a list of all the statements she makes about herself and her life through the course of the play, noting briefly in each case the *context* in which the statement was made. Taking Olga as an example, one might come up with the following sample list:

- 'I thought I'd never get over it.' (About her father's death.)
- 'I remember it all, as if we'd left only yesterday.' (About Moscow.)
- 'I felt... such an intense longing to go home.' (About Moscow.)
- 'I've already started to think like an old woman.' (About teaching.)
- 'All my strength and youth have been ebbing away.' (About teaching.)
- 'I'd have loved my husband.' (About her single status.)
- 'Yes, but it's cold. It's cold here, and the mosquitoes...' (About the locality.)
- 'That sort of behaviour depresses me, it makes me ill.' (About Natasha shouting at the servants.)

Reading these together, one might with justification conclude that Olga's driving need is *to go home*. Like most needs, this has a literal, an emotional and a sensual dimension. Olga would literally like to return to Moscow, her childhood home – which means that this need, if truly embodied, will give Olga a constant feeling of physical displacement and needing to be somewhere else. Emotionally, Moscow is also associated in her mind with a time of her life before the death of her parents, when she was happy and optimistic (and perhaps had marriage prospects). On a sensual level, Olga makes constant comparisons between the empty landscape around the town where she lives, together with the dullness of the town itself, and the vibrant and stimulating memories she has of Moscow.

It is not enough for the actor playing Olga simply to know what the need is. Using the text as her starting point and guide, she must also, through a process of exploration, construct the 'inner landscape' from which the need arises, using a combination of her sensual and emotional imagination and a range of appropriate stimuli. To grasp what this need is, not just mentally, but viscerally and emotionally, she needs to explore and internalise the following things:

- The story of Olga's life as she might remember it.
- The huge distance between Olga's provincial home and Moscow, and the contrast in lifestyle and sophistication.
- The emptiness of the landscape.
- The affluence and glamour of Moscow high society in the late nineteenth century.
- A sense of the new 'business class' rising up in Russia – in Olga's view, vulgar, insensitive, socially and culturally inept people, who are nonetheless growing in power and influence.
- A sense of the passing of the old Russia and the uncertainty of the future.

The actor playing Olga has to find ways of responding to these aspects of Olga's life both emotionally and personally. All actors have their own ways of doing this, but one of the most direct ways is through visual and aural stimuli. Music in particular can help an actor find a very direct connection between a character's situation and her own emotions. The important thing is to find pieces of music that can evoke specific aspects of the character's sensual world and the era in which she lives, while also stimulating an empathetic response in the actor.

If Olga's need is to 'go home', then her inner emotional landscape must encompass both the emptiness and dreariness of the landscape she is forced to inhabit and the contrasting idealised vision of Moscow. For the former, the actor playing Olga needs to explore stimuli that help her gain an emotional understanding of the vast cold empty region where Olga lives. There is much nineteenth-century Russian music, both classical and folk, which evokes precisely the kind of visual and cultural emptiness in which Olga sees herself. There is also a wealth of nineteenth-century Russian poetry expressing these same feelings, and much painting, such as the huge open landscapes of Alexey Savrasov or the birch forests of Isaak Levitan, which can offer an immediate visual sense of Olga's physical world and the emotions associated with it.

By contrast, the music of Romantic composers such as Tchaikovsky, who blend traditional Russian and Western European musical styles, can evoke the excitement and cultural vibrancy of Moscow in the 1890s. The actor playing Olga can build for herself an imaginary Moscow, romantic, passionate and artistic, which may not accurately reflect the real Moscow, but nonetheless becomes an essential part of her own personal landscape.

To make effective use of images, whether paintings or photographs, in the process of building the inner landscape, the actor needs to select and personalise. A landscape needs to acquire a specific place within Olga's world; the figures in a family portrait must be given specific identities. To complete this process of personalisation, an actor could create a scrapbook with Olga's commentary written on each image.

To make the most of the evocative potential of artistic stimuli, the actor might set up situations in which she can immerse herself in music and images, so that a process of daydreaming can take place. Creating a darkened space with candles or oil lamps, wearing the kind of clothes that Olga would wear, and filling the space with music, images and objects, is probably the best way of using these stimuli. The actor also needs to be precise about which point in time she is exploring within the narrative of the play, so that her imagination can work from the given circumstances of a particular moment and the preoccupations of the character in that moment. In other words, images and the associated emotions from the past need always to be in relationship to events and issues in the present (i.e. the text itself), otherwise the actor risks creating an emotional 'wash', which is passive and unspecific.

Research using artistic stimuli needs to be carried out in such a way that the work of art both arouses an emotional response in the actor, and also offers insights into how Olga might feel about specific aspects of her life at specific times. We can all be stimulated by music and poetry, but the actor must always distinguish between that which she responds to on a purely personal level and that which opens a door into another consciousness – in this case, Olga's. To do this she needs to keep hold of the important images in Olga's mind that arise at particular points in the text – the coldness and desolation of the landscape; the military balls that took place during her father's life; the musicians who play at carnival time; her father's funeral; her dislike of her job; her disappointment in Andrei, her brother, who was supposed to save the family and lead them back to Moscow, but lapses instead into gambling and mediocrity. As she searches for connection with Olga, the actor needs to seize upon those stimuli that seem to open doors into Olga's way of thinking and seeing, and this means always keeping in mind key moments within the text.

There is a danger here that the visual and aural stimuli by which the actor seeks to come closer to Olga's inner landscape may also evoke in the actor a strong aesthetic response, which may be almost too pleasurable. It is all too easy for the actor exploring Olga to 'fall in love' with her pain. This is certainly a risk, yet the same paradox might be said to characterise Olga herself. One might say that it is the very intensity of her emotion that makes her able to continue as she is. Her sense of physical and emotional displacement, and longing to be somewhere else, is perhaps a necessary antidote to the relatively dull life she leads. It gives her something to be passionate about, and allows her to avoid confronting what she actually is – a schoolteacher in a small provincial town who will probably never leave. On some level, then, one could say that Olga herself is in love with her pain!

The downside of this is that the actor may create an inner landscape for Olga that tends towards the self-indulgent and over-romanticised. To counter this problem, the actor also needs to employ the 'as if', in order to understand more fully the reality of Olga's life and situation, and the real inner pain for which her dreams are a foil and palliative.

To personalise the feelings she has accessed, using the 'as if', the actor playing Olga starts by making contact with her own emotional life, using aspects of Olga's situation to access real feelings in herself which help her connect her own inner landscape to Olga's. The choices she makes here will depend on her particular take on Olga, and the specific aspects of Olga's life and situation that arouse empathy within her. She might imagine herself, in her own life, somehow trapped in a cold empty landscape, far away from anyone or anything she loves or recognises, unable to find her way back. She might think about being stuck in a soulless, repetitive job. She might daydream about life with no partner or anyone who really loves her. She might imagine having to live, day in, day out, with people whose views and way of life she hates. She may have specific memories to help her access the feelings associated with each situation, but even if she doesn't, she can write stories in her head or on paper that take her to those possibilities. She can try to connect the music she has listened to with old memories and lost moments of her own. In other words, she finds the Olga in herself, not by making Olga the same as herself, but by empathising with a woman lost in a backwater of history, and by finding feelings in herself that mirror those of the character.

Once the inner emotional landscape starts to form, an actor is able to establish clear 'points of view' throughout the play, which are both specific to the circumstances and connected to the character's need. It is an exciting moment when, having done all of this work, you step into the space and start to apply the skills of reading and responding, allowing the inner landscape to become a deep resonator within which every spontaneous thought reverberates:

OLGA   We left Moscow eleven years ago, yet I can remember so well, how everything's already in flower in Moscow by this time, the beginning of May, how warm it is, and everything bathed in sunlight.

Even though Olga is not actually in conversation at this point, this, along with every other line in the play, still needs to be a *responsive moment*. In this case, Olga is responding to her sisters, who are there with her in the room – Irina excited and hopeful on her name-day; Masha buried in a book, mourning her dull life and marriage – and this speech is clearly a direct comment on them. Olga's objective is, of course, to awaken her sisters to what the family has lost, in order to maintain within all three of them the aspiration of returning to Moscow. Her need to speak comes from the moment, because although the sisters are together in the room, Olga perceives they are not, in that instant, mentally or emotionally connected.

Olga's 'point of view' in this moment derives from the gap between what she feels inside, and what she is experiencing around her. If the actor's inner emotional landscape is full of Olga's personal images and memories, then the words of the text will resonate within her like a sound box, and the audience will then both understand what she is feeling and thinking, and, in an instant, grasp the family predicament and the relationships between the sisters.

There is little more exciting to watch than actors who are both emotionally and imaginatively alive *and* connected to one another in the space. Very often in theatre we are treated to either one or the other, but Meisner demanded that actors should do both. We are not likely to be interested in Olga if she is continually lost in her own world and disconnected from the present moment, but at the same time we cannot fully understand or empathise with her unless we also understand her past and her sense of personal loss.

Avoiding Emotional 'Wash'

Later in the play, at the start of Act Three, Olga reproaches Natasha, her brother's socially ambitious wife, for shouting at Anfisa, their elderly servant.

OLGA   You know, you were so rude to Nanny just now... I'm sorry, but I just can't bear it... I felt quite faint...

This is a direct response to Natasha's treatment of Anfisa a few moments previously, yet Olga's reaction can so easily seem affected, overtheatrical and hysterical if the actor has not done enough preparation. It is important that the audience understands that this is not just a moment of disagreement or affectation, but an encapsulation of everything that Olga feels about Natasha's encroachment into the household, and indeed the whole ascendancy of the new lower-middle class.

At this point in the play, the actor playing Olga needs to be able to draw upon a mixture of distant and more recent memories – happy memories of her own childhood, when Anfisa was her much-loved nanny, and unpleasant ones of Natasha gradually gaining control of the household. She needs to have access to those memories and to be able to relive them, so that we understand this line of text not just as a reaction to a moment (though it is certainly that), but as a reaction from a very specific emotional 'point of view.' Olga feels faint, not just because Natasha has shouted at a servant, but because she can remember a time when that servant, as her nanny and second mother, was at the centre of her family life. Natasha's attack on Anfisa is therefore tantamount to a direct attack on Olga herself and her family. If the audience understand this on an emotional level, then they can both empathise with Olga in this moment, and gain a deeper understanding of the whole play.

To lay down these particular memories within her emotional landscape, the actor playing Olga can use a variety of stimuli, including improvisations, diary entries, or possibly old photographs. It is not difficult to find nineteenth-century photographic images of family life and childhood. Old photographs are always highly evocative and emotional objects, because they capture lost moments, and are thus linked to memory and recapturing the past, especially childhood. Working with real images of this kind, and building memories around the images, can help the actor playing Olga to find both a deeper connection with her need, and the clarity of thought and association that characterises this particular moment.

Once again, the actor also needs to make the link with her own emotions through the 'as if'. Few of us nowadays have a family retainer, but most of us can imagine how we would feel if an elderly parent or adored older relative was bullied and mistreated by a comparative stranger, perhaps in a hospital or care home. Spending some time in the daydream can help the actor to create these stories and use them to find a closer connection with Olga.

Mining the Text

Having dealt with this broad inner landscape, and having connected with Olga's need and the many memories and impressions that make up her past, the actor starts to attend to the detail of her scenes. She can do this by picking up and exploring the information in the text, and making clear creative choices in rehearsal, which help her to support her connection to the inner landscape.

Some of these choices relate to the activities outlined in the stage directions. For example, Olga's opening activity in the play is marking schoolwork, so the actor probably needs to know what the assignment was, how the students have responded, and how Olga feels about that response as she reads their work. The actor could even choose to make the marking of the books a specific contributing factor to Olga's opening speech. For example, if Olga had set the students a task to comment on a favourite poem of hers, and the students had responded in a lacklustre and uninspired way, that would both disappoint her and make her question herself as a teacher – which in turn would open up her underlying need and heighten her feelings towards the town, her father's death and her sisters. By finding and using an appropriate poem by Lermontov or Pushkin (two of the poets quoted in the text), the actor playing Olga can both connect with Olga's world by turning the task of marking into a real and significant activity, and make a creative choice of her own which brings her closer to the character.

A similar possibility arises in Act Three, when Olga is sorting clothes to give to the fire victims. Again, by making a choice about the precise nature of the clothes, the actor can lend a particular emotional resonance to the scene. Earlier in the scene we hear that among the fire refugees are children still in their nightclothes. So what if the wardrobe contained (among other things) clothes from Irina's childhood, which Olga had perhaps been saving for Masha or Irina's children but had never offered to Natasha? In giving the clothes to officers' children, Olga chooses to cut a link with the past, but at the same time ensures that the clothes go to people of her own sort.

A choice of this kind can provide a simple and direct connection to memories of Irina as a child, and of the happier years when their father was alive. When Natasha enters without knocking, Olga might feel embarrassed by the fact that she has kept the clothes hidden, and this immediately gives her another 'point of view' and a clearer context within which to play the dialogue. If Natasha sees the clothes, of course, she will understand immediately what is going on, and she too will start the scene with a clear 'point of view'.

It is important to remember that these are just *examples* of creative choices an actor might make, not instructions on how to play this or any other role. Your job as the actor is to make clear and specific decisions, based on the information in the text, which connect to the need and serve as doorways into the inner landscape of the character. The particular choices you make will depend to some extent on your own life experience. For instance, you might have to ask yourself whether the notion of giving away children's clothes has any resonance or meaning for you. An actor who herself has young children might make this choice because she can understand very clearly the emotional significance of giving away outgrown clothes, but this might not work for everyone.

The task, then, is both to find out the details and background of your character's life, and to be creative and exploratory in order to stimulate personal responses, and to arrive at a point where the detail of a scene is owned as much by you as by the playwright. You should always remember that the starting point for your creativity is the text itself. The idea is to pick up clues from what your character says and does, and then start to daydream.

Secrets

Meisner suggests that the key to playing certain roles, or rather, delivering certain lines, often lies in the actor making clear choices about secret circumstances in the character's life. These choices may never be revealed, even to the other actors, but they lend clarity to a line of text because they emerge directly from a piece of factual detail which the actor knows and has internalised.

For example, an actor investigating Olga's statements and attitudes cannot fail to notice her intense disapproval of her sisters' behaviour with men. Masha treats her husband with contempt and has an affair with Vershinin; Irina is, by her own admission, unable to love anyone. Olga continually scolds Masha, while trying to talk Irina into a loveless marriage with Baron Tuzenbakh. This aspect of Olga is quite puzzling, because it seems at variance with her rejection of provincial life and her dreams of something better. Looking further into the text, you can pick out the following intriguing facts:

- The character Chebutykin, a military doctor, was formerly in love with Olga's mother.
- He treats Irina as a daughter and she treats him as a father.

Putting these clues together, it is easy to come up with the idea that Olga's mother (whom Olga never refers to) was having an affair with Chebutykin, and that Olga knew. Given her feelings for her father, this would have upset Olga deeply. You could easily make this more specific by deciding that Olga had actually witnessed the infidelity, and that she had never told her father in order to spare his feelings. A secret of this kind would lend clarity and resonance to all Olga's statements about love and marriage:

MASHA   Oh, why not come out with it? I'm in love
         with Vershinin...

OLGA   (*Goes behind her screen.*) That's enough, I'm
         not listening to you anyway.

Secrets need to be selected with care, because it is all too easy for a secret to work *against* the text, or to set up irrelevancies that puzzle rather than intrigue the audience. The simple rule is that all secrets must come as *answers* to questions about the character, and what she says and does, which have arisen out of your text study. They must also fit the known facts, so that they support and give colour to the given circumstances rather than creating confusion.

Continuing the Journey

All of this work comes under the heading of emotional preparation, which, combined with the reactive skills derived from repetition, creates a metaphorical platform on which your journey of discovery in the space can begin. By allowing the inner landscape to interact with other actors in the moment, you stimulate impulses that tell your body what to do in the space. From here, as in most rehearsal processes, you begin to construct the physical and emotional shape of a scene by following impulses and seeing where they lead. Some of what you discover will become a permanent or semi-permanent part of your performance.

Some actors wrongly assume that nothing can be 'fixed' in Meisner, but this is not the case. Meisner actors have to accept many given circumstances, some of which pertain to the fictional world of the play, and others to the choices made during rehearsal. If you know that on a particular line of text you have to move close to another actor and put your hands on his shoulders (because you discovered this in rehearsal and the director liked it), then your job is to accept this gesture as one of the 'givens' of the production. However, the nature of the impulse that makes you perform the gesture may vary, along with the manner of performing it. In other words, you won't know until the moment of reaction precisely why you are doing it and how that feels.

Reading and Responding

Detailed emotional preparation and text work are essential pre-requisites for utilising your Meisner skills in the acting space. What you must remember is that the act of preparation and the act of responding do not exist separately from one another, but feed each other constantly through the rehearsal process and performances. When you start to rehearse, no matter how much preparation you have done, you will not immediately be able to respond from the character's 'point of view'. However, if you have the courage to trust your preparatory work and allow your discoveries to come from real interactions, rather than contrived or manufactured moments, then you will start to 'layer' the role. Each interaction will deepen your embodied understanding of the character, which in turn will enhance your ability to react organically from the character's point of view.

'Difficult' Roles

Some roles seem at first to be especially difficult to access, because the character's 'point of view' appears to be heavily influenced, not just by the life she has led and the experiences she has had over a long period of time, but by one or more heightened moments of trauma in the past. These were so intense and so specific to the particular circumstances in which they occurred, that it is very hard for you, as the actor, to reproduce them, or to understand how it might feel to experience them.

In Tennessee Williams's *A Streetcar Named Desire*, we discover that Blanche Dubois apparently spends a lot of her life reliving a deep trauma which occurred some fifteen years previously, when she discovered her young husband's homosexuality, confronted him with it on the dance floor, and then realised a few minutes later that she had driven him to suicide. The polka music ('The Varsouviana') from that moment repeats in her head throughout the play.

This presents an extraordinary challenge for any actor, because the particular past event that dominates Blanche's emotional inner landscape is so devastating and so complex. On one level, Blanche has experienced the betrayal of infidelity; on another she has failed either to perceive the truth about her husband or to empathise with his pain, and has thereby caused his death. The result must be a compound of personal loss, humiliation and unbearable guilt.

It would be pointless for an actor to spend time trying to reproduce in herself the emotions Blanche would have felt at the time these events occurred, for the simple reason that within the time frame of the play itself, Blanche does not experience these emotions as she might have done when the events occurred. The stories of her life are tragic, yet she seems to retell them with a kind of poetic fascination. All her past experiences are recounted with a kind of gothic lyricism, and everything she encounters she transforms in some way in order to stave off its essential ugliness. The view from Stella's window (an ugly, urban, industrial scene) is turned into 'the ghoul-haunted woodland of Weir' (an image from a verse by Edgar Allan Poe); the interior of Stella's drab apartment she glamorises with Chinese lanterns. It is as though she can survive anything except ugliness and stark truths. Her fear of being exposed by bright lights is both a metaphor for this and a literal terror of people seeing her faded looks as they really are.

As always, the actor needs to trust the text to give her the information she needs, and in this play she can find not just indications but very clear statements about how Blanche's inner landscape is formed:

> BLANCHE I'll tell you what I want. Magic! Yes, yes,
> magic! I try to give that to people. I
> misrepresent things to them. I don't tell the
> truth, I tell what ought to be the truth.

By her own admission, Blanche is engaged in a constant process of 'beautification' of everything within her life, which in reality is traumatic, devastating, humiliating or sordid. This simple piece of information is the key to playing the role. Blanche is not haunted by her past, because she has reconstructed everything within her past into fairytale and tragic romance in order to make it palatable. Even when she tells Mitch about her young husband's death, the story as she tells it is both poetic and dramatic – a retelling not a reliving. *Blanche's problem is not her tragic past but her sordid present*. Her struggle is not about coming to terms with what *has* happened, but about the immediate encounter with Stanley's harsh, modern pragmatism and his black-and-white notion of truth.

To realise this is to understand that characters in plays, like people in real life, rarely remember the past as it actually happened, but as a series of stories, images and emotional colours. This means that the process actors go through in order to build the inner emotional landscape is similar to the process we all go through in real life, as we assemble our memories into stories that can be told to ourselves or to others.

If you know this as an actor, then a lot of the stress of playing complex and tragic characters is removed. You may (and should) spend much time exploring the character's past and building their inner landscape; you may use the 'as if' to stimulate your own emotions and empathy. But the inner landscape you build, and from which you play the character, will not put you into a perpetual state of raw trauma – the act of remembering, in real life as in plays, is also the act of processing and reprocessing the past (and its associated emotions), so that, however painful they may be, life somehow still goes on.

The difference between real life and drama, of course, is that drama is very often about the points where the stories a character has constructed about the past come into direct conflict with the present. This is a dominant theme in drama, from the Greeks through to the present day. What this means for you, as an actor, is that your work only becomes genuinely truthful *in the reactive moment*, as the inner landscape responds to stimuli from the outside world. It is in those truthful moments that you really find your 'point of view'.

11

Meisner and Shakespeare

'Do all kinds of plays... hold on to the foundation of your technique'

Meisner and Shakespeare

Up to now, we have been working on text that falls broadly into the genre of realism. Realism by its nature seeks to give the illusion of real people speaking as people do in real life. In its later manifestations, this genre is characterised by its colloquial language and, in some cases, overlapping/disjointed dialogue that tries to reproduce everyday speech. As we know, this 'reproduction' is largely an illusion: if you examine the plays of David Mamet or Dennis Kelly you can see that, beneath the apparent chaos of the language, there is rhythm, poetry and lyricism, which enable the words to serve as conduits for the emotions felt by the actor. In other words, the dialogue is constructed in a way that dynamises the actor's imaginative connection with the character and with the objective, and keeps the actor emotionally active.

Iambic Text

Shakespeare's iambic verse is clearly not seeking to reproduce colloquial speech, since it is built on a regular verse form. What can be said is that the underlying rhythm of the iambic's alternate short and long stresses – which has been likened to a heartbeat – stimulates emotional connection. Further, the construction of his language shapes and directs the quality not just of what is expressed but what is felt and experienced by the actor who speaks the words.

Shakespeare and his contemporaries probably favoured the iambic pentameter as a verse form because that particular stress pattern occurs frequently within everyday speech. Examples like 'Why not come in and have a cup of tea?' or 'There's always such an awful lot to do!' are regular iambic pentameters which might pass unnoticed as such within a conversation, yet which have the same emotional directness and clarity as a line from Shakespeare.

Provided it is not spoken mechanically, and provided the stresses and pace are varied according to the meaning, iambic verse can actually sound uncannily like 'real' speech.

It could be argued, then, that Shakespeare in his time was doing precisely what Pinter, Mamet and other writers did later: writing heightened dialogue whose rhythms and sounds derive from everyday speech and stimulate the actor into a bodily connection with the text and with the other actors – which in turn tricks the audience into believing they are hearing something straight from real life.

The beauty of the iambic form is that once you have set it up as the basic underlying rhythm or 'heartbeat' of the text, the state of mind of each character can then be revealed by the nature and extent of their *divergence* from the regularity of that form. The language itself instructs the actor when to adhere to the regular beat and when to disrupt or reverse it; when to speed up or slow down; when to speak loudly and when softly; when to sound *staccato* and when *legato*; when to pitch high and when low; and when to *breathe*. In many ways it is like a musical score, and any actor attempting this text needs to understand its notation.

This may on the face of it seem to contradict Meisner theory. If the text is the canoe floating on the river of the emotion, then arguably you should not study its structure too closely beforehand but should allow it to emerge in the context of the scene. As a starting exercise, Meisner in fact often required his actors to speak the text without expression or meaning, to avoid the problem of a fixed interpretation.

However, with Shakespeare's iambic text it is both possible and necessary to operate a more analytical approach and to start by discovering the 'instructions' contained within the language, without going against the principles of the Meisner Technique. There does not need to be a problem or a contradiction with this, because actors in all aspects of their work have to work with a combination of the fixed and the variable. When working on a play you will always have to incorporate many predetermined circumstances that the text, the production and the space inevitably impose upon you.

The Meisner actor does not worry about these, but sees them just as another set of given circumstances, not of the fictional world but of the real world of the play and production. These given circumstances can include the 'givens' within the text itself. The Meisner actor does not try to go against the givens; you must always assume that even in that which is fixed there will always be variants, and those variants can and will be governed both by the actor's emotional inner life and by the truth of the reactive moment.

Some actors seem to have a very natural and instinctual understanding of the features of Shakespeare's language. They are able almost without thinking to identify and deliver the visual imagery, sound patterns and antitheses, and to maintain the underlying rhythm of the iambic verse in the face of shared lines and rhythmic irregularities. Others find this harder, but almost all actors find some aspects of the language confusing or obscure, and most find that the length and complexity of the thoughts demand maximum mental dexterity and breath control.

Delivering the Thought

In the example below from Act One, Scene Two of *Richard III*, Richard Duke of Gloucester is telling Lady Anne that she has made him weep even though he has never cried throughout the horrors of the recent war. To make his point he uses two examples of sad moments in the war – the deaths of his brother and father – and embellishes the second of these with a description of a whole group of people crying. All of this is contained within the body of a single thought, which means that the actor has to start the thought, put it to one side for eight lines of vivid narrative, and then vocally reprise it in a way that connects the end back to the beginning. The actor also has to find a way of contrasting two different stories within the eight-line narrative and giving them distinct emotional qualities, the first story being about the death of a seventeen-year-old boy and the second about the loss of the Yorkist leader and patriarch. The words in brackets are mine:

RICHARD
    (*Start of main thought.*)
    These eyes, which never shed remorseful tear –
    (*First story.*)
    No, when my father York and Edward wept
    To hear the piteous moan that Rutland made
    When black-faced Clifford shook his sword at him;
    (*Second story – change of tone.*)
    Nor when thy warlike father, like a child,
    Told the sad story of my father's death,
    And twenty times made pause to sob and weep,
    (*Additional image to strengthen second story.*)
    That all the standers-by had wet their cheeks
    Like trees bedashed with rain –
    (*Return to main thought.*)
                    in that sad time
    My manly eyes did scorn an humble tear;

And what these sorrows could not thence exhale,
Thy beauty hath, and made them blind with
    weeping.

It is clear from this example alone that Shakespeare's language
– or a lot of it, at any rate – requires a considerable level of craft
to be applied before its meaning can be released. Like a musician aspiring to play a complex score, an actor needs to learn
how to honour all the structures and devices of the text in order
to deliver its full power to an audience.

I do not believe that any of this work is at odds with Meisner
Technique. The musician who learns the notes, symbols and
instructions of a musical score will still be able to play the music
as no one has ever played it before, and, if this is an orchestral
piece, will be able to respond to the playing of other musicians
without departing from the composer's score. In the same way
you, the actor, can work flexibly within an embedded technique
which allows you to deliver the text in all its complexity while
also being spontaneous and responsive to other actors.

Meisner Technique is an excellent way of allowing you to
take ownership of text whose style may be a long way from your
normal speech, and whose form appears at first glance to allow
you less creative leeway than realist text. The point here is that,
however closely you have followed the 'instructions' in the text,
and however beautifully you speak the language, there will be
no truth or humanity and ultimately no clarity in your performance, unless you are both working from a truthful emotion
and allowing yourself to be genuinely responsive and genuinely
vulnerable to the other actor.

Meisner was clear that an actor should find an emotion
appropriate to the character's state of mind and need at the
beginning of a scene, and then allow the text to emerge naturally
on the 'river' of the emotional interaction. He insisted that the
text alone would not get the actor to an emotional climax or a
dramatic turning point within the scene with any degree of truth.

Particularisation

Shakespeare's text may offer you a great deal: the language can help shape the emotion, while the breath required to deliver complex thoughts helps to keep your voice resonant and your body open and responsive. None of this can take place, however, if the body starts from a closed place; if there is no emotional preparation to 'particularise' the character within your own emotional imagination and ensure that the person whom the audience sees within the scene is a living, emotional and reactive human being.

The difficulty here is that most Shakespearean scenes take place in worlds that are very far from our own experience. Taking *Richard III* once again as an example, you immediately come up against the problem that these characters express themselves in a way that is so alien to your own verbal and gestural language that you can easily fall into the false assumption that the characters of *Richard III* not only speak and move but actually *feel* things in different ways from a twenty-first-century human.

Meisner's 'as if' is a crucial tool for dismantling this assumption and bridging the gap between your own emotional life and that of a character in Shakespeare's drama. All too many actors seem to believe that the combination of a sort of 'generic' emotional state with the language of the play will somehow do the job, but this is simply not enough. Shakespeare's characters are like any other dramatic characters – they need to have specific feelings about specific circumstances, and their emotions and responses need to be particularised so that the audience can understand precisely who they are, what they feel and what they want.

Being Specific

Act One, Scene Two of *Richard III* opens with Lady Anne, a young woman lamenting over the corpse of King Henry VI – who, for political reasons, has been murdered by Richard Duke of Gloucester, presumably on the orders of his older brother, now Edward IV. Anne has been briefly married to Henry's son Edward, also killed by Richard, so Henry is her father-in-law. Anne's own father, the Earl of Warwick, has also been killed in the same year.

If we start by listing the key aspects of Anne's given circumstances, a picture begins to emerge which, although not contradictory to the simple idea of grief and bereavement, offers considerably more imaginative scope. Some of these circumstances can be taken directly from the text, while others are either historical facts or strong probabilities:

- At the time of this scene she is fifteen years old.
- She was married at the age of fourteen to Edward Prince of Wales, heir to the throne of England.
- The marriage was arranged by her father, the Earl of Warwick.
- She was in line to become queen at the end of Henry's reign.
- Her marriage lasted less than six months before her husband was killed, during which time it is doubtful that she and Edward spent much time together.
- She is now left friendless and devoid of political power. Her entire family has either been killed or died except her sister Isabella, who is married to Richard's brother George. Her father's estates have been confiscated.
- She has been given permission to accompany the body of King Henry, her father-in-law, to Chertsey Abbey for burial.

We then take another look at what Anne is actually *doing* in her opening speech, and we notice that, far from being in a state of collapse, she appears to be engaging in a very public display of grief, anger and invective. We glance back up our list, and the picture begins to form. This is a teenager who has been used as a political pawn, who has suffered massive bereavement yet does not feel safe to grieve quietly. She has deified her dead husband and father-in-law and is now giving vent to a very teenage demonstration of reckless rage and grief in an attempt to rouse public sympathy.

The actor playing Anne now experiences a revelation. She has been prepared to dig deep into her own emotions and imagine what it would be like to lose her partner and father in the same violent conflict. Yet the language of the scene does not support such simple, uncomplicated grief. It is full of anger, curses and accusation (even before Richard enters), with the result that the actor playing Anne admits she can't seem to connect up her own emotions with the text.

Gradually, this actor realises that it is not just grief that is driving Anne, but fear and loneliness, coupled with a deep anger at the way she has been treated. Her anger should really be directed at her father, but he is dead, along with every other significant male figure in her life, so she redirects her anger at those who are alive to receive it.

Keeping in mind that the 'as if' in Meisner is not based on an *actual* past event in her life, but on an *imagined* circumstance to which she has some level of emotional access, the actor playing Anne starts to search for an 'as if' story that works for her, and eventually she has it. Even the telling of it makes her cry. In her 'as if' world she has for many years felt unloved by her father, who has taken little interest in her, so she has developed a close (non-sexual) relationship with an older teacher, who has made her feel valued. While walking home one night, this teacher has been robbed and stabbed to death by a group of teenagers. We don't ask why or how she has arrived at this 'as if', because it is not our business, but the story clearly has some resonance for her.

The emotion here is very different from that of her previous 'as if'. Here, feelings of abandonment and anger mix freely with the grief, yet the actor understands very well how all the anger she has felt towards her father over the years will now be redirected onto the killer of the surrogate father-figure.

The actor playing Anne spends a little time in the daydream, fleshing out in her imagination the details of her 'as if' story until they are so vivid for her that the emotion is showing clearly. She takes the daydream right through to the moment of the stabbing as she imagines it, focusing on the expression in the eyes of the killer.

To help her get a physical sense of death, I then ask another actor to lie on a table as if dead, his hands crossed over his chest, and tell the actor playing Anne to try and wake him. She does so gently at first, and then with increasing desperation, until she is shaking the body so violently that it begins to shift on the table, an arm falls off the edge, and eventually the body is lying half on, half off the table, looking like a murder victim just after the event.

She realises what she has done, and tries to get the body back on the table, but she is a small woman, and the male actor a muscular six-footer. She struggles with him until eventually I send on two servants to help. Without a word, they shift the body back into position. The actor playing Anne then painstakingly rearranges the body into a dignified position and crosses the hands back across the chest.

The purpose behind all of this is two-fold: firstly, it sets up a physical and emotional relationship between Anne and the corpse of the dead king; secondly, it allows her to engage in a physical struggle which opens the breath and lets the emotion live in the body.

By the time we start the scene, Anne is a mass of confused emotions and physical sensations. I tell her just to speak the text in context, and a strange thing happens. The confusion vanishes, and the emotion finds an outlet through the words and feelings contained in the text. The text shapes, defines, directs and stokes the emotion so that we are able to follow Anne's journey from the body to the killer and back again. Again, the bracketed comments are mine:

ANNE
  (*Public respect for the King.*)
  Set down, set down your honourable load,
  If honour may be shrouded in a hearse,
  Whilst I awhile obsequiously lament
  Th' untimely fall of virtuous Lancaster.
  (*Pity for his death.*)
  Poor key-cold figure of a holy king!
  Pale ashes of the house of Lancaster!
  Thou bloodless remnant of that royal blood!
  (*Self-pity.*)
  Be it lawful that I invocate thy ghost,
  To hear the lamentations of poor Anne,
  Wife to thy Edward, to thy slaughter'd son,
  Stabb'd by the self-same hand that made these
      wounds!
  Lo, in these windows that let forth thy life,
  I pour the helpless balm of my poor eyes:
  (*Sudden rage.*)
  O, cursed be the hand that made these holes!
  Cursed the heart that had the heart to do it!
  Cursed the blood that let this blood from hence!
  More direful hap betide that hated wretch
  That makes us wretched by the death of thee,
  Than I can wish to adders, spiders, toads,

Or any creeping venom'd thing that lives!
If ever he have child, abortive be it,
Prodigious, and untimely brought to light,
Whose ugly and unnatural aspect
May fright the hopeful mother at the view;
And that be heir to his unhappiness!
If ever he have wife, let her be made
More miserable by the death of him
Than I am made by my young lord and thee!
(*Return to formality.*)
Come, now towards Chertsey with your holy load,
Taken from Paul's to be interred there;
And still, as you are weary of this weight,
Rest you, whiles I lament King Henry's corpse.

What this actor gives us is a curious mixture of emotions, but this is not the ritualised lamentation of a bereaved daughter-in-law. In the first part of the speech, it is as though Anne is trying to contain herself and express her grief with a measure of decorum. When we get to the line 'Be it lawful that I invocate thy ghost', it is as if a much less controlled and childish grief bursts out of her, and the speech becomes about her loss and her loneliness. This quickly turns to blind rage, and at this point she loses control completely, giving herself over to a hatred that finally dissolves into sobs. By this time she is on the floor. Gradually the sobs subside, she recovers herself and orders the servants to lift the body and continue the journey.

This actor has worked from her own emotions, not in a generalised way but through a very personal understanding of what it feels like to be abandoned and alone, and to use anger as a defence. Because she has begun the speech in a state of emotional preparedness, the language has taken her on an unforced emotional journey.

She has also allowed herself to respond to the presence and stillness of the dead body. Dead or not, her Meisner training has taught her to stay outwardly focused and responsive to those around her. The invocation of King Henry's ghost comes as a very real moment in which Anne seems suddenly to understand that the corpse can neither hear nor respond. From this point she speaks not to the body itself but to Henry's spirit, so that when she lets her tears fall onto the wounds, this is a demonstration to the spirit in the surrounding air, not to the body, although the failure of her tears to heal the wounds brings her attention back to the body's emptiness.

I ask the actor playing Anne what she thinks her objective is in this part of the scene. She thinks for a moment and then says, 'To make the world admit that this is all wrong'. We see at once what she means. After decades of conflict the nation is so relieved to have the 'glorious summer' of peace and a stable monarchy that the 'war crimes' of the House of York (which include the summary execution of prisoners after the battle of Tewkesbury) are being brushed under the carpet. Anne, as one of the last survivors of the House of Lancaster, is one of the few people brave and desperate enough to keep the issue alive.

Avoiding Cliché

The actor playing Richard has to go on a different journey. As with Anne, we make a list of the given circumstances of the character at the start of this scene:

- At the time of this scene he is nineteen years old.
- His brother, King Edward IV, is twenty-nine.
- He has a physical disability which does not impede his ability to fight but makes him socially awkward and (he believes) unattractive to the opposite sex.

- Having given his all to the war in support of his brother, he is now marginalised and unpopular.
- Although in Shakespeare's version of the story (see *Henry VI, Part Three*) he was one of the killers of Edward Prince of Wales, it was actually his brother Edward of York who stabbed the young prince first.
- Like Anne, he is one of the few people not happy with the post-war situation.

The actor playing Richard notes that the emotion driving him to seek power by whatever means stems directly from Richard's personal sense of exclusion, especially from the world of courtly love. In this play, and in *Henry VI, Part Three*, he is continually taunted for his disability, which is seen by others as nature's warning of an evil disposition.

The 'as if' here is quite a simple one. For this actor it is as if, despite trying his hardest, he has been continually starved of love, respect and approval; despite not being any worse or better than his siblings, he has always got the blame and always been taunted about his looks.

The feeling that emerges is one of a universal contempt and loathing for humanity reminiscent in the modern day of the Columbine killers. As with the Columbine killers, it is unhelpful to start with the notion of an 'evil' person. The actor playing Richard needs to get inside this character and feel his starting emotions, otherwise he is likely to end up playing a pantomime villain.

Most people can recount experiences in which they felt excluded, mocked or unjustly judged. Meisner 'as if' work is not usually about digging into one's own past, but imagining scenarios in one's present or future that might produce a feeling similar to that of the character. In this case, the actor comes up with two scenarios that could easily happen in his own life. In the first of these he invites a lot of people to a party, possibly for his birthday, and not one person comes. To compound this, no one thinks to call him and make an excuse. He is left sitting on his own, surrounded by carefully prepared food and drink. He tries to call a couple of people but gets only voicemail. After waiting an hour he picks up a bottle and smashes all the plates and dishes, sweeping the debris onto the floor.

I ask the actor which image within the scenario is most evocative, and without hesitation he says it is the food and drink. Somehow the idea of lovingly preparing food for people and having it rejected affects him deeply. This might not be so for all actors, but the 'as if' has to be about finding a personal connection – the particular image or event which stimulates *this* actor into an emotional response.

The other scenario is where, as a child, he makes a piece of jewellery for his mother in a metalwork class, in a desperate attempt to gain her approval. She looks at it with disdain and asks him why she would want to wear anything like that. Later he finds it in the bin.

Back to the play itself, we then do an improvisation in which a series of characters, including Richard's mother the Duchess of York, Henry VI, his brothers and various others, give their view of him as if they had all been able to be part of an inquiry after his death. None has anything positive to say, even when pressed. Throughout this the actor playing Richard sits and listens.

By the end of this, the actor reports that he feels an over-whelming sense of rejection and worthlessness. I ask him where that is going to take him – will he kill himself or fight back? After a moment he says he will fight back.

I ask him to read the first speech of the play, and he does so with clarity, comprehension and emotional intensity which allows us to understand perfectly the dehumanising journey Richard goes on. What becomes clear by the middle of the speech is that Richard is asserting a moral position for himself, which is that if society offers him nothing then he owes society nothing. His bitterness becomes the excuse and the driving force for everything that follows.

Returning to the dialogue of Act One, Scene Two, I ask the actors to name the objectives of the two characters at the start of the dialogue section. The actor playing Anne replies that she wants to shame him, first publicly, so he will get out of her way, and afterwards more deeply, so he will take his own life. The actor playing Richard says that he wants to soften her so he can woo her. However, he is puzzled, because as he rightly says, he has just explored the bitterness of Richard's existence, yet the character doesn't appear at all bitter in the duologue. I agree with him and ask him why this might be. He thinks for a moment and then says, 'It's because he's stopped caring – he can do anything now.'

This realisation is very important, because it reminds us that the 'as if' leads us to the underlying emotion, but the text and the events in the space can alter that emotion out of recognition. In this particular scene, this actor's 'as if' reasserts itself at the end through the bitterness of Richard's final soliloquy, so it is essential that the actor has visited those emotions beforehand.

We play the first part of the dialogue, and it comes out like an awful cliché. Richard's compliments so clearly lack sincerity that they just infuriate Anne further, while her ranting has no effect on him at all. We don't get as far as the turning point of the scene, because I can't bear the prospect of watching the actors force a moment they have so clearly not reached.

I ask the actors to remember their earlier Meisner work, and to let the determination to pursue the objective be constantly affected and shaped by the other actor. I remind them that only by establishing a connection can either of them hope to achieve their objective. They are both anxious, because, as they say, if they make themselves vulnerable to one another, they may fail to achieve what the character wants. I point out that we already know that one character wins and the other loses in the end. How the scene ends is not the issue – how that ending is reached, and how the audience understands that journey, is the really important thing.

They start the scene again, and this time Richard allows the sincerity of Anne's anger to affect him, so that his lines start to resonate with genuine admiration and a sense of his own unworthiness. Anne is taken by surprise and there is a moment when she almost weakens, but the text helps her out. There is a long section in the scene where almost everything she says is just his previous line twisted into antithesis and flung back in a way that is almost stichomythic, except that these are not just single lines but two or three-line speeches, as in the following example (which is reminiscent of a repetition exercise!):

RICHARD

> Vouchsafe, divine perfection of a woman,
> Of these supposed crimes to give me leave
> By circumstance but to acquit myself.

ANNE

> Vouchsafe, diffused infection of a man,
> Of these known evils, but to give me leave
> By circumstance to accuse thy cursed self.

In the context of Richard's charm offensive, this comes across as a defence mechanism, which allows Anne to hide behind mockery and anger rather than risk betraying her vulnerability. Yet both the group and Richard are able to perceive the fragility of her defences as line after line is flung back in this way, because by making her lines dependent on his she hands him control of the dialogue.

The actor playing Richard decides in that moment that he must play the scene as an actor would – in order to prove a villain he has to play the lover, not villainously (which would fool nobody) but with commitment, desire and sincerity. This comes naturally out of the 'as if'. The actor playing Richard concludes that if he had lived for so long without any kind of affirmation or approval, then he would have learned to generate his self-esteem from within, not from others. Therefore Richard can allow himself genuinely to desire and admire Anne in this moment, because he knows that even if he fails he will have lost nothing.

What we now start to read from Richard is adoration of Anne and vulnerability to her, so that every insult makes him want her more. His eloquence now seems to be coming from an emotional place rather than from a superficial desire to manipulate.

We are now able to see the scene organically unfolding. Many actors and scholars have puzzled about this scene's conclusion, wondering how such a complete turnaround could be achieved. Yet the actor playing Anne now experiences first-hand what it feels like to try and maintain anger for someone who visibly adores her and appears to be in a state of moral confusion as a result:

RICHARD
> Your beauty was the cause of that effect –
> Your beauty that did haunt me in my sleep
> To undertake the death of all the world,
> So I might live an hour in your sweet bosom.

ANNE
> If I thought that, I tell thee, homicide,
> These nails should rent that beauty from my cheeks.

RICHARD
> These eyes could not endure that beauty's wrack;
> You should not blemish it if I stood by.
> As all the world is cheered by the sun,
> So I by that. It is my day, my life.

ANNE
> Black night o'ershade thy day, and death thy life!

Anne maintains her anger for most of the scene, but for the most part she is not able to fuel it from Richard himself – so it is only a matter of time before she 'runs out of steam'. The actor playing Anne reports that she feels an increasing urge as the scene proceeds to respond emotionally to him, and only the given circumstances, her starting emotion, and the text itself prevent her from doing so.

Richard senses her weakening, and opens himself to her moment by moment until, by the time the long speech is reached, he is himself openly emotional while Anne appears spent and exhausted. This is because he has been able to energise both his ardour and his despair from her treatment of him, while she has had to deal with the dissonance of two conflicting feelings – anger and neediness, which have drained her energy.

As watchers in the group our position is clear. The first time the scene was played, we were unable to believe that any version of the journey the text tells us must take place was actually taking place within the minds, bodies and emotions of the actors. By contrast, the second time it mostly makes sense, because the actors have thrown away their preconceptions, trusted their technique and the text, and are prepared to find their way through the scene without pushing or forcing any moment. From here the possibilities for exploration are endless.

12

Meisner Ongoing

'Meisner Technique is the only tool we have that can genuinely get us out of our heads and into our bodies and emotions'

Meisner Ongoing

Meisner Technique can broadly be divided into two main skill areas: *reading and responding to other actors* and *emotional preparation*. The first can be acquired through the continuing practice of repetition exercises; the second requires a combination of technique, common sense, imagination and personal courage.

Meisner's insistence that the actor needs to *particularise* and to *personalise* in order to gain emotional ownership of a role is something actors need to return to again and again. It is a simple idea and a simple technique, yet all too many actors take for granted that they already understand a character (which they may do intellectually), and don't take the time to find where the feelings of that character sit within their own emotional life. I believe that any company of actors needs to maintain a culture and a language of emotional investigation, in which actors feel safe to explore their own emotional responses and to understand themselves as artists more fully.

Any actor can learn to read and respond to others, yet all too many actors find that this aspect of Meisner Technique makes them feel too vulnerable and exposed, and they shy away from it. It is certainly true that to master Meisner Technique, an actor must first believe in the necessity of truthful interaction, and then work hard to instil the habit of openness into his everyday modus operandi.

The Meisner Technique cannot be a part-time practice. An actor who genuinely believes in its precepts and efficacy, and wants to place it at the centre of his craft, needs to practise repetition in all its forms throughout his career. By so doing he becomes a better actor and a better student of human nature.

HOUSE OF GAMES
Making Theatre from Everyday Life
Chris Johnston

THE IMPROVISATION BOOK
How to Conduct Successful Improvisation Sessions
John Abbott

THE IMPROVISATION GAME
Discovering the Secrets of Spontaneous Performance
Chris Johnston

IMPROVISATION IN REHEARSAL
John Abbott

INVENTING THE TRUTH
Devising and Directing for the Theatre
Mike Bradwell

LETTERS TO GEORGE
Max Stafford-Clark

THE RELUCTANT ESCAPOLOGIST
Adventures in Alternative Theatre
Mike Bradwell

TAKING STOCK
Philip Roberts and Max Stafford-Clark

WORDS INTO ACTION
Finding the Life of the Play
William Gaskill

www.nickhernbooks.co.uk

facebook.com/nickhernbooks

twitter.com/nickhernbooks